Buying "THE" House

By Stephen Sapphire

Forward

Buying "THE" house.

Not just any house, YOUR HOUSE!

Your FIRST house.

This book is designed to help you survive buying your first house!

It can be a scary adventure - Spending more money than you have, more than you have ever spent before, making a really big commitment.

There is risk in buying real estate, you can and may lose money, or you can and may profit from it.

You should want to be the BEST BUYER when you make your offer.

If other people can make it through the process, so can you!

I wish you the very best for your future!

Good Luck.

Disclaimer

By continuing to read this document, you agree to the contents of this disclaimer.

This publication is NOT professional advice, it is merely designed to provide topical information about the subject matter covered with the understanding that the publisher and authors are not engaged in rendering real estate, legal, accounting, tax, or ANY other professional advice and/or services and that the reader agrees to proceed at their own risk.

Buying or selling Real Estate is not something that everyone can or should do. Persons who buy or sell and/or invest in real estate MAY and DO lose money from time to time. You too may lose money in real estate.

IF you do not understand what you are doing, what you are signing, what you are buying, what you are selling, what commitments you are making or experiencing in a real estate transaction you should obtain professional help from an attorney, realtor, loan agent, geologist, engineer, home inspector, and/or many other professionals available before you proceed.

If real estate, legal, or other expert assistance is required, the services of a competent, professional licensed person should be sought out by you in your geographical area before you enter into any deal. Sign nothing unless you fully understand and agree with what you are signing. Your licensed realtor is who can advise you.

Our limitation of liability, if any, to you is a refund of the cost of this document.

Effective date 1/21/2022.

Table of Contents

Forward	2
Disclaimer	3
How do people Buy the House?	5
How to create a personal budget plan	9
Sharing the load	16
How much home can you afford?	18
Renting vs. buying	20
How to decide where to buy a home	23
How to pay for a home	26
How a mortgage works	29
Let's talk about the downpayment	31
When to buy a home	33
What is Real Property	35
How Realtors get paid	37
How an appraisal works	44
What make a home valuable?	54
How to find a house to buy	63
What to look at when touring a home?	73
Questions I ask during the showing	82
What NOT to do when touring a home	87
Everyone's role in real estate sale	91
The Home Buying Process - High Level	105
Loan Types	106
What is a Full Doc Loan?	117
How the loan process works	121
Some Real Estate Terminology	122
The Offer	135
Inspections	137
After the close	141
The home buying process – Detail	143
Reviewing your credit scores	147
How to improve your credit score	153
In conclusion to all the above	171

How do people Buy The House?

Houses today are very expensive.

How do everyday people achieve the goal of home ownership?

Start with having a job, have financial discipline in your life to prioritize, save money for a downpayment, get approved for a mortgage, shop for and Buy THE House!

What will a house cost in 20 years?

History indicates residential real estate (a house) will cost at least twice what it is worth today in 20 years.

Houses today are expensive, but they will most likely continue to go up in price.

A house is a major investment, you should think of treating it as an investment.

With the recent rampant inflation, all the products needed to build a house have gone way up in cost, driving up the cost of new homes.

There is, and will continue to be a housing shortage. The population will continue to increase, and more people enter the buying side of the housing market every day.

There is a large shortage of waste water treatment facilities, fresh water reservoirs and water sources, and then there is the lack of available land to build on.

Many communities practice NO GROWTH policies, designed to keep prices high. Whenever we have a big issue in the housing market, congress helicopters in and fixes it - the last thing any elected official in Washington DC wants is THEIR home value to drop.

The housing market in many ways is a protected system, regulated overtly and covertly.

The bottom line is, over time, housing costs will continue to rise, as will wages.

So, let's talk about how you prepare to "Buy THE House", that will be YOUR HOUSE!

Firstly, it starts with planning and financial discipline…. Unless you have super rich generous parents that are gifting you all the money to buy anything you want, you need to start with planning. If you do have a sugar daddy funding your home, stop reading this book now - LOL

Most of us do not have, did not have a wealth advantage. You can still get there from here with hard work, knowledge of how the process works and good financial discipline.

First you need to examine your personal finances…. Only YOU can manage your personal business, and you should manage it LIKE A BUSINESS!

First, know your Income vs. Expense   You need to earn more than you burn!

If you do not have a written budget that you follow, the next chapter is for you.

If you do have a written budget, do you reconcile it at the end of every month?

If not, the next chapter is for you, it's very important to "keep score" with your finances by comparing your assumptions of expense by category to the actual amount you spent – this is called reconciliation, and it's fundamental to a real budget.

When you apply for a home mortgage, or a pre-approval that results in a letter of approval from a lender for a specific real amount of money they are willing to loan you towards a qualified property, the lender is going to look at your finances with a microscope.

Sounds scary, but if you are organized, and you know your numbers, it's not that hard to move forward.

You need to save money. Saving money for a down payment takes time. Save enough money to have some reserves in a savings account that is secure and will be there when you need it for your downpayment. (i.e. - not bitcoin or any other wild eyed crypto scheme)

How to save money? You put a line in your personal budget that is the amount you can afford to save each month from your income, AFTER you pay your bills, transfer this amount to your savings… don't spend it!

Improve your credit score   - There is a chapter later in this book that details how to do this.

Lower your monthly expenses - Pay down debt, avoid large new purchases on credit, buy that new car AFTER you close escrow on the house.

Look back at the last few months to see what you spent your money on… read your bank statements and credit card statements, do you really need all those streaming content memberships?

What did you spend that can be eliminated going forward? The less you spend, the more you can save.

Calculate potential tax savings – Later in this book, I touch on how buying a home can save you thousands in Income taxes. You should have a conversation with your tax person or a CPA to learn how this will affect you specifically.

If you do your own taxes, you can do a "what if" with your last years return to estimate the effect buying a house will have on your situation.

Once you have cleaned up your credit, or at least learned what your credit scores are, and saved some coin for the downpayment, then you will want to get pre-approved for a Mortgage, which will tell you what you can actually afford!

Do this BEFORE shopping for The House!

Pick your lender of choice carefully, applying more than once will lower your credit scores.

Once you have saved for a down payment and become pre-approved for a mortgage, you are ready to start finding the house you will buy!

So, read on – lot's more to go!

How to create a working personal budget plan

It's a proven fact, having a written personal budget is an effective way to build wealth.

Regardless of how much you do or do not earn, best practices are to manage your personal business with a written plan that you RECONCILE after each month to make sure your assumptions and estimates are correct

Many people "live to their means", a saying that simply means they spend every dollar they earn, every month!

When I first created a written budget for myself, I listed my known monthly obligations and debts, totaled them up and was pleased my income exceeded my monthly debt.

So, end of month, why was I broke?

Time for a deeper dive. I took all my (then) many credit cards, my bank statement and downloaded everything into Excel, and that total blew my income to bits! I was spending way more than I was earning yet I "thought' I was being responsible, but I was not.

So, what to do? The first thing I did was consolidate to one credit card, the one with the best cash back deal, and I worked to pay it off.

Second thing I realized was that if I did not compare what I spent to what my written budget was, I would be lost as to my actual financial position.

My cash back card pays 2% - on everything – so I realized that if I put all my recurring bills on autopay for that card, I'd earn 2% free money! In the process all my transactions are in the same place at the end of the month, making it easy to download into Excel.

The important thing here is to PAY 100% of the statement amount ON TIME IN FULL so there is NO INTEREST charged by the bank on the credit card.

I now do this every month.   When I started, I had several credit cards opened with balances. I opened a new cash back card just for this while I worked for a few months to pay off the other accounts.

I have found the best budget method is the written budget, I keep mine in Excel so my computer totals things for me.   The most important part is the end-of-month reconciliation. I download or print out all the transactions in my bank (debit-card) account and my cash back credit card account.

I then take my written budget (Sample layout below) and enter in to the spreadsheet the total for each category.

What this does for me is helps build financial discipline. When I am over on a budget item, I am

11

the one to blame for it, and I am the one who can correct this going forward.

When I examined my personal spend, I found lots of small items, that after a months' worth of indulgence, really add up…. Like Starbucks… monthly amount $350…. Wow, I did that? I'd rather skip the Starbucks and put that money somewhere else – Like my savings account.

What I learned when I first downloaded my previous month's actual spend, was somewhat shocking.

It was so shocking to see what I spent my money on that I downloaded the previous 6 months and it was even more shocking…. I was spending an average of $1200 a month dining out!

I needed some "financial discipline" if I was ever going to save money to buy the house.

I made changes, real changes. Every month I update my spend on my spread sheet to measure my goals.

It feels really great to not only know that I am withing my budget, but also know that I am financially moving forward!

I encourage the reader, take a look at how I laid out the budget spreadsheet.

Customize your written budget for your monthly expenses, keep a miscellaneous for one off's.... like a birthday gift, extra stuff you bought from Amazon, etc.

If you need ideas for what your categories should be, look at your last 6 months spend.

Be very honest with the amounts you put in.... If you list an amount for food... and you're always over, you can adjust it up.

Then add a column for each of the 12 months.

I call this reconciliation my "scorecard", I measure how I do to keep inside my budget.

If you have debt, work to pay that off as quickly as you can. A proven debt reduction method is to overpay the smallest debt first while you make minimum payments on the rest of your debt.

Minimum payments take YEARS to pay back. But if you overpay each month as you can, your success will be much faster.

Reducing debt is great, but it only really works if you reduce your spending and stay on a budget.

When you reduce debt, it will help your credit score, and make your life easier.

13

Below is a Sample of a written budget – Note the scorecard for your results to the right of your monthly budgeted amounts.

You should have the other 9 months to the right in your spread sheet.

IF you do not have excel, you can also just write this on a sheet pf paper, the important thing is to measure your results each month against your assumptions in the budget.

You will find this very helpful, interesting and informative.

My Written Budget   2024

Expenses

Category	Estimated Monthly Amount		January Actual	February Actual	March Actual
Rent	$	2,000	$ 2,000.00		
Electricity	$	135	$ 128.50		
Credit Card Debt	$	350	$ 362.00		
Water	$	45	$ 47.20		
Auto Payment	$	456	$ 456.00		
Auto Insurance	$	140	$ 140.00		
Gasoline	$	250	$ 312.00		
Auto Maintence	$	100	$ -		
Food	$	600	$ 710.00		
Dining Out	$	400	$ 289.00		
Travel	$	250	$ 190.00		
Miscelanous	$	250	$ 295.00		
Money To Savings	$	500	$ 500.00		
Monthly Total	$	5,476	$ 5,430		
Monthly Variance			$ 46.30		

Income

Full Time Job	Estimated Monthly Amount		January Actual	February Actual	March Actual
90,000 annual net takehome is	$	5,250.00	5250		
Other (investments)	$	260.00	261.25		
Total Income	$	5,510.00	$ 5,511.25		
Income vs. Expense	$	34.00	$ 81.55		

When your circumstances change, like you have saved your money, got your finances in order, and Buy THE House, update your budget accordingly.

As you get ready to buy, you can make a "Pro-Forma" budget that basically is a "looking forward" budget wherein you can estimate your new expenses after you Buy THE House…. In essence make a budget before you buy to make sure you can afford THE House before you move.

Sharing the load (without arguing)

This all sounds great, now what if you have a Spouse, life partner, etc. that you are combining financial goals with?

We all know, the number one thing couples argue about is MONEY or money-related issues.

If you have no financial structure in your relationship, you have left your relationship wide open for this kind of trouble.

My wife and I have never had one argument, 28 years not one…. Why?

We both had argued with our Ex's to the point we just do not want to argue any more – that's no way to live, and certainly does not help going forward.

When we started co-habiting, we implemented structure day one.

We discuss and both agree on all major purchases, if we both don't agree to the spend, we don't make the spend.

You have to have a unanimous quorum, respecting both parties.

In our case, as is often the case, one of us earned quite a bit more than the other, so we took that into consideration and split the expenses, literally.

I paid the rent, car payment, insurance, my wife paid the electricity, water, cable TV / internet, and food. These items fit our earnings.

We each had our own budget that reflected our own responsibilities, keeping our own accounts and with the way we divided the expenses, we both could make the needed payments with our respective income.

With this method, we never fight over money as there is never anything to fight about.

We each have our budget, and our own money to pay our allotted part of the monthly expense.

Sharing the load without arguing, only works like this if both parties respect each other and want to do their part to have a healthy financial future.

17

Saving for a down payment for a house can be stressful if BOTH partners do not agree. Take this into consideration, don't set unrealistic goals and you can succeed.

How much home can you afford?

This is the first question most people have, and many have no idea how to answer it.

When you buy a home with a loan, called a mortgage, you are going to live with the monthly payments for many years.

It is important to most buyers that they are comfortable with the amount of the monthly payment.

The question stands, how much home can you afford? It's not a hard answer, in fact it's pretty simple if you know the formula.

The people who back mortgages determined the formula is: "Not more than 28% of your combined GROSS income."

Example:

One spouse earns $100,000 per year and one spouse earns $50,000 per year thus their combined income is $150k.

$150,000 X 28% = $42,000

$42,000 Divided by 12 is $3500 per month.

Therefore, if you buy a $700,000 Home,

your down payment will be $140,000.,

your loan will be ~$560,000.

Today's rates are about 6.75%

Expect about $12,000 of up-front closing costs

Your mortgage payment would be ~$3632. per month Principal and Interest plus, about $841 per month for "Insurance and Taxes" (also known as PITI)

So, in this example you are all in at ~$4473 per month.

Using the above formula, IF your gross income is more than $134k per year, then this mortgage should be affordable.

If you buy a less expensive home, your cost goes down, more expensive it goes up. - You get the idea.

IF YOU ARE NOT COMFORTABLE WITH THE COST OF A MORTGAGE PAYMENT, then do not sign the deal, after all you are the one who will make all those monthly payments.

If your income as in my example is $150,000 a year, and this seems like a payment you cannot afford, you might need to look at where your money is going… perhaps review your budget and your spend…. Never commit to a payment you don't think you can make comfortably.

Renting vs. buying

Right now, renting is arguably much more economical than buying.

So why do people buy a home?

When you buy a home, you pay a price for that home. Often a homeowner gets a mortgage loan to pay for the property in monthly installments.

When you buy a house with a mortgage, say a conventional 30-year fixed rate mortgage, your last payment in 30 years will be the same as your first payment.

You may have heard the term "House Poor", referring to people with home ownership costs that render them "poor"?   A bigger fear is the phrase "RENT poor".

Ask yourself, "How many times higher will your rent be in 30 years?" At least double if not quadruple.

Buying a home "stops" the cost of housing inflation. You buy a house for 900k in 2024, in 2054 it will be worth many times more, but your monthly cost will be the same if you have a conventional 30-year mortgage.

What a mortgage does for the homeowner is assure them that in the future their monthly cost will be the same.

What will your landlord do, every year?

Essentially, buying a house, vs. renting, can be a great hedge against inflation, reducing your risk of higher costs later in life.

Owning a home can also be a great tax deduction for many people as at this time "Mortgage Interest" you will pay is 100% tax deductible.

Additionally, up to $10,000. A year of the S.A.L.T. is 100% deductible.

S.A.L.T. = State and Local Taxes

SALT includes Property Tax, but to take this deduction, you need to own a house, not rent. It needs to be "Real Property" and you need to live in it as your primary residence.

Talk to your tax advisor to see how this will affect you BEFORE you buy a house.

In many cases this can save HUNDREDS to THOUSANDS of dollars a month off your federal income taxes, thus effectively offsetting your mortgage cost.

Owning a home historically has been a great hedge against inflation. As prices rise, wages rise and usually so do home values. Over the last 10 decades, home values have multiplied.

Owing your home is part of the American Dream, it creates stability for you, your family and your neighborhood.

Only you can do the math to determine if it works for you, but owning a home has been a reliable way to build wealth.

Some things to be aware of – rent vs. own, renting often includes water, sewer and trash fees. As a homeowner you will pay these yourself – you may have to make a deposit on these services as well (usually like a hundred bucks) when you first open your account when you close escrow on your house.

Some houses have more or less utility services - such as Natural Gas, Electricity, etc.

Water is usually $100 or more a month.

Trash pickup can cost between $20-$80 a month, depending on where you live.

Sewer – sometimes included with water, sometimes billed separate.

You should ask the realtor or go to the water department's website to see what these items cost per month.

Something in your rental home breaks - you call the landlord and they pay to fix it.

Things break in your own home; you get to pay for the repair.

Homeowners pay property taxes, landlords build it them into your rent.

There are different expenses in Owning vs. Renting.

How to decide where to buy a home

Buying a home is, for most people, the biggest purchase of their lifetime.

It is not like buying something at a store where you can change your mind and return it if you decide you don't really want to buy it.

All the legal documents that you will sign give you, as buyer, ample opportunity to decide not to close the deal, and they also make sure you know that once it's done and closed, it's closed.

Now, this does not mean you cannot sell your property to someone else, thereby getting rid of it, but when you are using a loan, almost all loans have covenants and huge penalties if you sell within the first year or 2.

Home prices vary city to city, street to street, state to state. So how do you start to decide where you want to buy?

For starters you should to take into consideration the location(s) of your income sources – i.e., your Job Location.

Many millions of people commute a bit, or a lot, to have the ability to buy a home they can afford. In the California market, a 2–3-hour commute is pretty common.

Take a look at any freeway pointed into Los Angeles or the Silicon Valley or the SF Bay Area any weekday morning and you can see millions of people commute.

Perhaps by commuting, one spouse might be able to stay home with infant children. With the cost of daycare, especially before age 3, it's often cheaper for one spouse to stay home.

This should be considered when you start a family, as even in a perfect world, the birth of a child will impact your income. If you are relying on both parents' income to make ends meet, it can be catastrophic.

Many people buy a home in an area where they have a support network, family, friends, church, etc. and then commute to a higher paying job.

An early question you should resolve to help your home search is how much commute are you willing to do?

Many times, when faced with a big decision, you may find it much easier to decide what you WILL NOT be willing to do, thus exposing the options you will be willing to do.

Learning the entire home buying process, hopefully by reading this document, will help guide you in to the correct order of events in order to succeed.

Part of what you will do is get qualified for a loan. This will identify for you exactly how much of a loan you can get, and this may limit the options of where you can buy.

When you are looking at a house with a realtor, the realtor cannot legally tell you that it's a Good or Bad neighborhood.

That's not legal, it's discriminatory – and professional realtors won't go there.

However, since you are deciding if you want to live in a neighborhood you might want to do some investigation on your own if you don't know the area.

One type of question you can ask the realtor is "Does this part of town get a lot of police calls?".

The number of police responses to an area is factual, can be informational and not discriminatory.

You also can find a huge amount of demographic, economic, and statistical background information about any city in the United States at https://www.city-data.com

Once you have decided where you are willing to buy, how much you can afford and what effort you are willing to undertake to make this work, you are ready to start searching for a home.

How to pay for a home

Unless you have very wealthy and generous parents, or have been born into a large trust fund, or have won a lottery, or won a large lawsuit, or received a large inheritance, or landed a large amount of wealth by some other such very fortunate situation, you need a loan!

A loan that is used to buy real estate is called a "mortgage." A mortgage typically is secured by the value of the property, meaning if you don't pay your payments, they legally seize ownership of the property securing the mortgage.

If you default (don't pay the payments), then the mortgage holder (lender) takes legal action called a foreclosure and seizes the property, transferring it into their name to recover their investment.

You obtain a mortgage from "Mortgage lenders, mortgage brokers, banks, savings and loans, credit unions, direct lenders, angel financiers, etc.".

Most common is a bank type financial institution or a "DIRECT LENDER."

Do a web search for "Direct mortgage lenders" and you will find plenty. Working with a Direct Lender Online usually means you will pay less fees and have more clarity since everything they do is in writing on your computer screen for your review.

To get a mortgage, you must "qualify", meaning you need to have sufficient income, clean enough credit and clean enough payment history.

You also usually need some seed money that is called a "down payment".

Your downpayment, often 20% of the properties purchase price, is what collateralizes the loan, meaning you have put your money into the property so the loan to value starts at 80%.

This means you have something to lose, giving you an incentive to pay, and if you do not pay your mortgage loan payments, most likely the lender will get their investment back if they have to foreclose on the loan, repossess (take) the house then sell it.

You do not want this to happen, so you will happily make your mortgage payments on time and in full each month!

This is why lenders want you to have some money in the property so you're also at risk.

Typically, a "Conventional Mortgage" (Conforming) is one initially valued at less than $647, 200 and requires 20% down.

Getting pre-approved for a Mortgage will tell you what you can actually afford! Do this BEFORE shopping for The House!

How a mortgage works

Albert Einstein once described compound interest as the "eighth wonder of the world," saying, "he who understands it, earns it; he who doesn't, pays for it."

Another time when a reporter allegedly asked Albert Einstein "What is the most powerful force in the world?", Einstein purportedly instantly answered "Compound Interest!"

I'm not sure after all these years if either of these accounts are true, but I can say compound interest is an amazing thing.

A mortgage Loan uses a methodology of calculating compound interest.

Compound interest is when the interest one pays on the unpaid principal balance of a loan is calculated before the payment is credited thus providing the lender interest up to the payment date.

A mortgage uses this method of compounding interest on the unpaid principal every month before any funds are applied to the principal borrowed.

Example -   You obtain a mortgage for $300,000 at 4% Interest over 30 years with a payment of $1,520.06 per month.

From the table below, only showing the first 3 payments (there are 357 more rows of payments until the example mortgage is paid in full), you can see how the interest is compounded upon the principal, then the principal applied thus reducing the balance.

Payment #	Balance	Interest	Principal
1	$300,000.00	$1,125.00	$395.06
2	$299,604.94	$1,123.52	$396.54
3	$299,208.41	$1,122.03	$398.02

All "young" mortgages are heavily weighted towards more interest than principal in the beginning, thus if you want to expedite the full repayment of your loan, any additional principal you send will accelerate the payoff.

Most mortgages are never paid in full by monthly payments. Often the original mortgage is paid off during a re-finance or property sale.

Let's talk about the down payment

Most mortgage programs require you to put some cash into the purchase, this is commonly referred to as the "down payment".

In a "conventional" loan, the standard MINIMUM amount is 20%. Some people put much more than 20% in as down payment. Obviously, the less you borrow the smaller the monthly payments, the less interest you will pay, and the more equity you will start with in the house.

Typically, when you apply for a loan, somewhere in the process before approval, the lender is going to ask you "what is the source of your down payment funds?".

This is an important question, more important is the answer.

Always be honest with your answers on loan documents, however thinking ahead is a good idea.

If you saved your down payment from your salary over the last few years, then that is the answer to the question where did you get your down payment - i.e., "from earnings"

If you won the funds, say at a casino, lottery or playing crypto markets late night, your lender will assuredly want to see it listed on your tax returns showing you paid the income tax due, if any.

If it was a gift from your parent(s), depending on the size of the gift they may want a letter from the giftor stating it is a gift, and not a loan and further stating that all income taxes have been paid on behalf of the gifted amount.

Currently in 2022 per IRS, the annual Gift tax Free maximum is at $16,000. – If your parents give you say $100k for your down payment, you should consult a tax professional first to know exactly where you and the giftor stand tax-wise so you can accurately and honestly answer the lenders' question.

Let's say you have a 401K, that's brimming with funds – there may be a temptation to do an early withdrawal. This will trigger penalties and taxes; it can be very expensive – I suggest you get some professional advice from a CPA before you raid the 401k piggy bank to understand what it is really going to cost you.

Most 401k's allow you to borrow money against the balance you have saved.

If you borrow from your own 401k funds, when you repay the funds to the 401k you will pay interest. HOWEVER, since you "essentially" loaned yourself the money from your own 401k, the interest that you pay goes to your 401k, i.e., back to yourself.

The fund charges a small fee each month for handling the transactions, but most of the interest goes into your 401k as you repay the loan.

This "MAY" be an option, however before you proceed, talk to your lender, see how this affects your numbers, see if they have heartburn with this that will kill your loan before you take action.

Also talk to your 401k administrator and learn exactly how this works for your plan.

Talk to your CPA too to see if this will cause any tax issues or other unpleasantness.

When to buy a home

Short answer, anytime you are comfortable with the property you have found and the price you are going to pay for it.

However, Residential Real Estate is generally seasonal in many parts of the country.

Wintertime, Rainy Season, Holiday Season, whatever winter is to you, it's not the popular time of year when people List, Sell and Move. If you are shopping in the winter season, you may well be discouraged. Just wait for spring.

For every Buyer, there is a seller, and the sellers move when convenient. Most sellers once sold, must find a place to buy.

OFTEN Sellers sell property contingent upon their ability to find a place to buy, or your ability to sell your old house to fund the purchase.

These are called "Contingencies" and they refer to anything – all sales using a lender (mortgage) are contingent upon loan approval.

Spring, starting late February to early April is when many new exciting worthwhile properties will be listed. If you are a serious buyer, you should get ready to buy in the spring and/or summer.

In the winter you find stuff so bad that no one wants it, and sometimes a real gem.

Estate sales, where an owner has died and their estate is being settled by probate or by an attorney executing the instructions of a trust or the decedents will can happen any time of year.

35

Estate sales are usually as is, something to consider.

But generally, for me –

I "Think Spring" for the best opportunities.

What is Real Property

What will and won't qualify for a mortgage

"A stick-built home" IS real Property and is the phrase that refers to the usual and ordinary home most people live in, it does not arrive in one or 2 premade pieces, it is built on-site (i.e. – Built with sticks of lumber hence the phrase "Stick Built") with permits and you own the land under it.

A Mobile home is not real property – IF a mobile home is set on land you own on a permanent foundation where you own the land under it, you might be able to get a home loan.

A mobile home set in a park, where you have a monthly rent to your landlord, is not considered real property. They do these with auto-type loans.

A Modular home, set on land you own, on a permanent permitted foundation is real property and will qualify for a loan – However they often appraise very poorly.

A modular home where you do not own the land, and you pay rent to stay on the land, is not real property.

A Condominium, where you own a share of the land and a share of the building, is real property.

An apartment you rent, or a house you rent, is real property for the building owner (landlord), not you as a Tenant.

Fractional Ownership is where you buy a small or large fraction of a property – for purposes of this document, I will not include this option…. And you cannot get a mortgage for fractional ownership as conventional financing.

A "Time Share" is not real property; however, it is the most recognized worst investment on the planet – just google "timeshares as investments" for lots of insightful views.

How Realtors get paid

Realtors get paid as follows:

(it's usually not negotiable unless the property being sold is a very expensive property)

Selling Agent 2%, Selling Broker 1% for a total of 3% to Selling agent/agency

Buyer's Realtor gets 2%, Buyer's Broker gets 1% for a total of 3% to the buyer's agent/agency.

Example In a $500,000 deal -

The buyer's realtor gets 2% or in this example $10,000. and the buyers' realtor broker (boss) gets 1% or in this example $5000

The seller's realtor gets 2% or in this example $10,000. and the sellers' realtors' broker (boss) gets 1% or in this example $5000

Therefore $30,000 total commission is paid by SELLER from proceeds of the sale.

SO, this is IMPORTANT - you will want your happy offer to find its way to the TOP of the pile and be attractive to the seller so they pick you to buy their house.

When you find a house, you want to look at in person, CONTACT THE LISTING AGENT. If you make an offer using the listing agent, you can find some advantage.

Some listing agents will not represent both parties in a sale, in this case you may have to find a different realtor. Look for an experienced realtor that has a clean record.

You can check their license record at your states website where they control realtors' licenses. Google will find it for you.

Now, by both seller and buyer using the same agent, there are some things the realtor will not be able to share with you, mostly around the price and price negotiating.

If you are using the listing agent, they will not disclose private information like telling a buyer what the seller's bottom line price is even if they know it, that's illegal and not ethical, BUT would they tell you anyway if they were not the listing agent? Nope.

When both seller and buyer use the same agent, there will be a legal form that you both will sign that details the restrictions that this situation creates.

For me, personally it's not been a problem, it seems to be easier to get things done, get more information faster about the property and…

IF you use the seller's listing agent as your agent, then they earn both seller and buyer agent commission. On a $500k sale, they would get $20,000 commission vs. $10,000.

Realtors will NOT tell you this, they cannot legally solicit this, but in the real-estate industry it's called a "Double Ender" when an agent gets both ends, and who would not want to get paid twice as much?

Getting paid twice as much commission, although they will not say this out loud, is a motivator. Realtors love double enders when they are the listing agent and the buying agent.

IF the BROKER sells a property and gets both ends, they get all 6%, or $30k.   trust me, this will help your offer.

We ALWAYS try to buy with the listing agent, also known as the seller's agent and have found it very helpful, here's why:

The seller's realtor reviews all offers before they are submitted for consideration by the seller, so they know what the other offers on the table look like – they cannot tell you what they say,

40

BUT they will guide you as in, let's say the house is listed for $700k…. they may "suggest' you over bid at $725K.

Realtors are well paid, successful ones are smart, and very busy, many will simply not write an offer that they know is too "weak".

This is another "tell" if your agent is the listing agent that your offer's too weak and they don't want to write it up at the price you are requesting…. but again, they will not lose their license and overtly disclose info between buyer and seller.

Sellers usually want to know a bit about the buyers, but they do not usually want to meet you. They do not want to waste their time on buyers who cannot perform. MANY sellers don't want to sell to people that their neighbors (friends) might not like, some just want highest dollar, most simply do not care who buys their house.

To most sellers a BIG priority is to pick buyers that will not create a follow-on lawsuit so they want "good" buyers. What's better than "a nice pleasant newly married first-time home buying couple starting a new family in their wonderful home"

That's the story you want the agent to sell to the seller… and using the listing agent, the story can be told. Some of the offers will be cold-hearted investors who just buy and sell, and many sellers don't like these type buyers as they know we all have attorneys.

You will have time to inspect the home, pull records, look in the attic, basement, etc. after your offer's accepted, JOB ONE IS GET ACCEPTED!

In CALIFORNIA, BUYERS can cancel for no reason right up to the close of escrow. Your realtor will put language in the contract that allows this, as it is the law, so don't over think the offer, you just need your offer to get accepted.

When I say buyers don't usually want to meet you, there is always an exception.

We bought a stunning estate quality property a few years ago, actually built by the original owner as his wife's dream home. The wife had passed, and the original owner was moving on yet his primary interest in selling was to see his home went to someone he approved of.

His deceased wife had inherited the property, and he had her dream house built on it. 70 mile view, 5 acre gated estate quality property. The owner had the home built from the ground up, 3 story and he spent

42

WAY more than it was worth, and he was more than a bit attached emotionally.

He was also 86 years old, very spry and very active, a wiry guy - retired US Navy brass, he did not beat about the bushes with conversation.

He also had a strong Alabama accent that put a wonderful emphasis on his directness of speech. He was NOT the least bit politically correct nor shy.

When we went to see the house a second time, he was there waiting. The movers had just loaded up his grand piano and he told us it was headed to his son's house in Phoenix.

He then very directly asked us if we had a serious interest in his home, I said we did, he said "Good."

Then he told his realtor (also his nephew) to take the other "salesman" outside somewhere and amuse yourselves while I talk to these people. The realtors exited to the deck so we were private.

Soon as they were outside, he says, "Now, Son, If you folks would be going to church, exactly what kind of a church would that be?"

I shared with him my church preference.

He said, "Goood. Now, if you people were to vote, how would that go?" I told him our political preference, and he said "VERY good".

He told us part of his life story starting age 16, his career in the navy during WW2, his love of the game of golf, about his deceased wife, the property, the historical items on the property – 5 artesian springs one mine shaft all left over from California's 1849er Gold Rush days.

Then he shares his belief his nephew, also his realtor the guy now out on the deck, was in his words "an idiot, and the house was way overpriced, and that it had been on the market 4 months". He told us what he thought it was worth.

Then he looked out the window a minute, and said, if you folks are thinking about making an offer, this afternoon would be a good time before I change my mind.

When the realtors came inside, our realtor asked him where he was moving to since his wife died and he was selling the house.

He looked at our realtor and says, "MOVING? I'm not moving, I done got married, I live down there" (pointing to a house below us), and then he says "I'm 85 years old, I aint got time to waste!"

We wrote and submitted an offer that afternoon. Our offer was $160k under asking, the amount he said he thought it was worth.

He accepted our offer instantly.

My point is I don't suggest avoiding the owners, it's just not common that they want to know the buyers before the business is agreed upon.

How an appraisal works

How is a home's value established?

After you make an offer, and it's accepted, your lender will order an appraisal – to make sure the home they are buying you, has sufficient value to secure their investment.

BUYERS pay for the appraisal, UP FRONT, separate from the loan.

COST OF APPRAISAL - Most appraisals these days cost $750 to $2000.

You BUYER, AKA "The Borrower", pays the appraisal cost UP FRONT, even if the house does not appraise high enough, and you do not get a loan or if you are denied a loan.

If you pay for an appraisal and it fails, your $$$ are gone and so is your loan.

VA loan programs have much more complicated appraisals and cost at the high end as most appraisers do not do them. A VA appraisal includes testing every burner on the stove, light switches, furnace, etc., There are many fewer appraisers that are VA certified as it's another level of complexity and liability to them.

Many appraisers today are backed up 4-12 weeks, they have lots of work, every re-finance and purchase using a loan requires an appraisal.

In some rural areas, it can take a while and sometimes cost a bunch more to get an appraiser to spend the travel time to get to and from the subject property.

Some sellers won't wait for an appraisal as time is money. If you follow our suggestions below, the realtor you choose will be able to guide you i.e. – If the seller wants cash buyers only, this is not the house for you.

If you are a buyer with a loan, the deal is on hold until the appraised value of the property collateralizes the lenders position, so the deal goes nowhere with your loan until the appraisal is favorable.

This delay costs the seller money, if the seller's proceeds are $500k, and they have to sit 60 days, they continue to pay expenses on the property, and lose investment opportunity on their proceeds… so it's common today for experienced sellers to say "cash buyers only"

In California, A licensed appraiser will be selected from "the pool of appraisers" for the county that the property is situated in.

You, your realtor and your lender will generally have no control over the selected appraiser. The realtors are no longer allowed to share info with the appraiser.

All the appraiser will see is publicly available knowledge, like the listing price, but the appraiser will have no idea what your offer is, and therefore no idea what value is needed.

The appraiser will schedule a time with the seller's realtor to have access to the physical property. They use a standardized format to document their inspection of the property.

This inspection is for VALUATION only, it is not about defects or needed repairs, unless it's a VA loan, and then they basically test everything in the house for "working order", i.e., everything in the house must exist and be in working order.

If the house has no stove, or no refrigerator, then the VA appraiser cannot test its working order, and the appraisal fails.

If you are doing a VA loan, let your realtor know when you tour the property.

The appraiser measures every room; they measure the outside. They note the lot size, lot features, quality of construction, key features, upgrades, roof type, foundation type, etc. to create a profile of the home.

All residential appraisals use the UNIFORM APPRAISAL method, that is documented on the standardized Uniform Appraisal Report. This way all sales are done same-same, and everyone knows how to read the report.

Basically, there are 3 competing ways to value property. The appraiser will pick the one of these 3 methods that best fits the appraisal they are conducting, using the phrase "Highest and Best Use" of the subject property.

These 3 appraisal methods are:

"Cost approach,"

"Sales comparison approach,"

"Income capitalization approach."

The Income Capitalization Approach
is for RENTAL property

It's also a pretty simple formula, usually in most markets, "Rent times 120 months = base value" of a rental home.

Example a rental that rents for $2500 a month is worth $2500 * 120 = $300,000 (base value)

The Cost Approach
is for NEW CONSTRUCTION ONLY -

Example total cost of building a new home

Example – If when the appraiser adds together the new homes construction costs + sales costs + lot cost + any site improvements and it totals $667,000 – Then the cost approach appraises (values) the property at $667k

The Sales Comparison Approach is what usually will be the "highest and best use" for a primary residence appraisal - i.e. your new home.

To apply the Sales Comparison Approach, the appraiser will pull 3-9 comparably similar

49

homes to the one he is appraising in the immediate vicinity that have sold (and closed) in the last 90 days that are most comparable in his opinion.

The appraiser then builds a comparison table in their software that results in the "Standardized Uniform Appraisal Report" as a PDF.

What they come up with is what other houses sold for per square foot. Although it's a subjective process, meaning subjective as to the appraiser's opinion, in the macro it's pretty accurate AND whatever value he comes up with will be the value the lender uses to determine if they fund the loan.

If you are buying a weird property, like say one with 2 (or more) houses on the same lot, the appraiser will have to look farther away from the subject property to find a comparable, and this can affect the value dramatically.

Many people think, oh, 2 houses on the same property means double the value. But it does not work that way.

From an appraisal perspective one of the 2 houses is deemed the primary residence and the second usually smaller is deemed an accessory unit, often valued at a simple maximum of $10,000.

For appraisal purposes, and in the comparative process all comparable's will have an accessory unit also, valued at $10k.

Beware of weird properties – spring boxes, mine shafts, creeks, culverts, tall retaining walls, etc. can and do affect the value.

An old inground pool can easily be a liability.

If there is a hot tub on a deck, your homeowner's insurance goes up.

A loan will not be funded if the property is not worth, determined by the appraisal, what your offer was.

That is; the value of NOT just the loan amount, but the property value as in down payment plus loan must be equal to or less than the appraised value.

Now, let's say you have an appraisal, and it's not good. What can you do?

You can complain, argue, waste time. Appraisers almost never change their opinion, they dig their heels in as if they change their opinion, then they take on liability.

You can also take the option of getting a second opinion, but that means paying for a second appraisal.

I had a house appraised once; the appraisal came in "low", too low for the loan.

The appraiser was from out of the area, and did a very sloppy job.

In fact, he indicated in the written descriptions of the subject property that the house had no garage, but yet included in the photo section of the appraisal a photo of his truck parked in the driveway in front of the garage.

Options for correcting this oversight to get my mortgage to complete this purchase?

Buy a second appraisal….

Then you get into the game of competing appraisals and then the lender gets very nervous, they will tend to lean to the lower one, so it was game over.

We lost that buy as the appraisal killed the deal.

The appraisal is very important to the entire loan and home purchase.

After your offer is accepted, an appraisal is ordered, you then pay for the entire appraisal fee up front.

Appraisal companies prefer you flip a credit card for speed of payment vs. write a check.

This is important to understand since you are paying for the appraisal up front!

If you are buying a home for, let's say $500,000.   And you are putting $100,000 down or stated differently 20% (of $500,000), the home needs to appraise for $500,000 or more.

Let's say it appraises for $475,000. And your accepted offer was $500,000.

Let's also say you have the ability to up your down payment to $125,000. – as a strategy to make up the missing value in the appraisal....

Your lender will NOT fund a mortgage on a property that does not "appraise".

Why?

Because they do not have an 80/20 loan to value ratio, what you do have is a property that did not appraise, game over. Options here are to ask the seller to lower the price.

Sometimes this works, unless it's way out.

I sold a property once; the appraisal was $3000. low, it was not worth the time and energy to re-start the deal and waste another month, or two finding a new buyer, so we lowered the price $3,000. and made the deal happen for the original buyer.

Communication is key to getting things done.

Your realtor handles all the required forms, signatures, etc. in these situations. It's important to retain a professional licensed realtor with a reputable firm.

As an example;

In a conventional mortgage, you need 80/20 Loan-To-Value. That is 20% down payment to an 80% loan value. For an $800k home you need the house to appraise at $800k!

If you offer $800k for a house, and it appraises at $760k…. Most likely the deal will die.

Options to cure this type of appraisal deficiency are, seller reduces cost or buyer puts in a bunch more cash, but the lender will not pay more than a house is worth, so adding more cash is usually a non-starter… and the seller most likely has a back-up offer and wants a quick sale as time costs the seller money.

Getting a favorable appraisal is important.

About 20 years ago, my wife and I actually got permission from a seller to go in the day before the appraisal and clean up the house we offered on.

The house was empty and had been for a year or more, so it was a bit buggy and dusty with fogged up windows, spider webs and the like.

54

We cleaned floors, washed windows, spent about 2 hours making it look/smell better.

The appraisal came in ok for value, but the appraiser noted "rot" on one window, and our loan evaporated in minutes.

A backup, all-cash offer was accepted, and "our" home was sold to another buyer.

IF the house does not "appraise", your deal is dead, and your appraisal fee is lost.

Again, a favorable appraisal is very important!!!

What make a home valuable?

Usually, there are 2 (TWO!) main things that determine a home's value.

Location and Size

Location, Size – in that order are the primary price influencers.

These two things, location and size are the main influencers of value, the rest is fluff.

Granite counters, tile floors, those are nice things but they amount more to selling points rather than big value items. Want more value?

Add a room! A 20x20 room addition @ $200 a sq ft can add ~$80k

Yes, the appraiser will take into consideration things like a nice kitchen with nice stone counters, but the reality is almost all houses today have nice kitchen counters – so in the comparable process it adds little to nothing.

When the appraiser selects comparable's to determine value, they will look for houses with very similar features, as in recently remolded, view, pool, etc.

The most valuable thing is the LOCATION, usually.

I say usually here because there are one-offs, like a famous person once lived in the house, or a famous architect designed it, or a gruesome murder took place in the home years ago….

These "one-offs" can mess with value up and down, but generally, "location" is a key metric to valuation.

You can change everything about a home except you cannot change its' location. Corner lots, busy streets, no view, next to a church, (Churches are wonderful but very noisy) an industrial area, a dangerous bad neighborhood, etc.….. Not good.

The best way to judge a neighborhood is look at the other homes that have SOLD, ask yourself if you would walk down the street at night alone?

Would you like to see your children walking to school on this street?

If your kids are school age, you might want to find out how is the neighborhood school?

If school is important to you, go say hi at the local school office, see for yourself what you think, how you feel about your kid's future in that school.

You should take the time to get to know what matters to you about where you will live. If you are planning an addition to a house, go talk to the local planning department, find out if you can do what you want to do.

Are you commuting? How will that be in relation to the house you are looking at, imagine the commute, even maybe do a dry run.

Time and distance have a cost, is it something you feel is worth doing?

Remember, you can change many things about a home, but not the location – the location is paramount.

The other thing of value is the SIZE of the home.

The size of a home, technically known as GLA (Gross Living Area) is the amount of square feet of LIVING space… garage does not count, storage shed does not count, separate cottage in back yard does not count as GLA.

GLA is contiguous living square feet under the roof of the primary house.

A primary tool of an appraiser will be to measure up the square feet, and multiply by the average of the "comparable's" in the immediate area of the home's location

A view lot vs. no view can add 25k to 250k or more. A 30-year-old pool can reduce the value, obvious dangerous situations and unfinished rooms can cause an appraisal to fail.

You DO NOT want to buy the cheapest, ugliest, most run-down house in town. At a later date when you want to sell your house, you will be selling the cheapest house in town.

A home with an "In-Law Cottage", "Granny Flat", detached rental, second house, etc. on the same lot can be a good thing, but it must be understood.

The salesman (realtor) may hype this as a source of income, place for your mom, or your 27-year-old living at home still, but in any event, this is technically referred to as "an accessory unit" to the appraiser.

Quite often a second home on the same property can reduce value as in the comparable appraisal process the appraisers often have to go a considerable distance away to find a house with an accessory unit and thus the location comparable part may be skewed not in your house's favor.

MOST appraisers will attach a value of $10,000 to the accessory unit. That's it!

It may be a wonderful modern second house on the property, but if it's not part of the primary residence it's technically, for an appraisal called an "accessory unit".

You may think having the appraiser assign a $10,000. value to the accessory unit (i.e. – the second house on same property) will reduce the appraisal value, but not really as when the appraiser selects 3 comparable properties, he will select 3 with accessory units as well and tag each of them as being worth $10,000.

Most everyone wants a fixer!

Buyers swarm "fixers".

If they are in the right location, investors will gobble them right up. Some "Fixers" are problem properties, and you really need to know what you are buying.

No one wants to own a money pit!

Foreclosures often are sold much cheaper as the lender is really only trying to recover what money they can. Foreclosures can be very tricky, risky and really hard to understand what you are buying as often they are sold before the door is unlocked. I have always avoided foreclosures.

Often, quite sadly, in today's world when a homeowner is disgruntled with their mortgage, broke, unemployed or maybe suffering illness or addiction, they will damage the house before their eviction is done.

If you cannot inspect the foreclosure thoroughly, you should avoid it.

Things that commonly happen to foreclosures are; the previous owner who is losing the house to foreclosure because they did not make their payments, might tear out all the kitchen cabinets and sell them.

They often sell the appliances out of the house before they leave, sell the bathroom fixtures, and it they are angry with their situation or lender, it's not uncommon to find the toilets have been poured full of concrete destroying the plumbing under the house and foundation.

Since the people being foreclosed upon are technically the property owners, they can do what they want with their house until they legally give it up.

A foreclosure can be a major money pit, may not appraise, may not qualify for a loan… so if you are looking for a house you can move into, you may want to leave the foreclosures to somebody else.

The cheaper it is, the worse it is. Sometimes they are sold sealed bid, sight unseen. BEWARE.

Again, if you cannot inspect the foreclosure thoroughly to understand what you are buying, you should avoid it.

A house is an investment, remodels are expensive in time and money. Better to pay a bit more and get something nice so it will appreciate better for you, and you will enjoy your time there more…

REMEMBER THE VALUE IS IN THE LOCATION AND SQUARE FEET!

Example – If you have a 2400 sq foot home selling for $700,000 that is $291.66 a sq foot.

When you look at a home in the same area, and its 1925 sq feet and they are asking $690,000 that's $358.44 a sq ft.

You need to find out why this difference in cost per square feet exists.

There are thousands of investor buyers, they are your competition.

Most investor buyers have cash, so they can avoid the appraisal, buy problem properties (Fixers) and close quickly.

Sellers want to close quickly as they are responsible for the property taxes, payments (if any) up to the date the sale is completed, referred to as "closing escrow".

If the seller has a $3,000 a month mortgage, every day costs him a hundred bucks, so sellers usually want sales to close sooner rather than later.

Personally, as an investor, I look at my target markets every day – it's a pulse of the market type thing. I like to keep up with everything selling; the how, where and what of it.

EVERY DAY – this is the type of diligence it takes to find that pearl of a house amongst the junk. I have a realtor.com search set to send me anything new in the areas I am interested in, with the key features we like.

About 20 years ago, a friend of mine invited me to dinner in at his club in The O.C. – On the way to dinner, he says "I need to stop by my house – Hey, I'll show you my 500 sq foot 2-million-dollar home".

It was a very nice little place, in a very nice neighborhood, very well appointed, clean, gourmet kitchen, but only 600 sq feet. In these 600 square feet were a Kitchen, Bath, Bedroom and a Living room.

This house was so small they had a projector TV mounted up high on one wall that projected the TV images on the opposing wall of the living room as there was no space for a TV.

The very small front and back yard had been paved with beautiful Mexican tile and had a built- in barbeque so they could entertain.

One really valuable feature to my friend's house was that you could open the back gate and walk down to the private dock in Huntington Beach Harbor where my friend keeps his 53' boat.

It was an incredible location, indeed a very powerful location.

The value of this house is the location, obviously not the size. Bigger homes in the area often sell for $10 to 20M and more, so at $2M it's really a cheap home for the neighborhood.

It's important where you buy, as most likely someday you will sell your investment, and you should consider what makes your home valuable to your future buyer.

How to find a house to buy

OK, so some naïve people think you just find a realtor, and tell them what you want, and they will drop everything and find you a home!

It's a bit more complicated. Most realtors don't have time to shop for you. Most realtors are very busy, highly successful people who have a lot going on.

Many realtors only focus on getting seller's listings, as that is a sure commission. If you are the listing agent, it does not matter who sells it, you get paid the listing commission.

Young to the industry, inexperienced agents have more time… but way less experience.

I have found the best success as a buyer by contacting the listing agent of a house AFTER I find the listing myself on Realtor.com

I have found the listing agent usually knows more about the property and the sellers than anyone, this can be an advantage to you, as well as the listing agent for many reasons.

Options – You have many different ways to find a new home as today there are many advertising methods used to sell a house.

From yard sign to the online, printed ads, real estate guides, MLS, live realtors, virtual realtors, even Craigs List has a Real Estate section.

In today's world most everything is bought and sold online, Real Estate is no exception. Online sales are ideal for this industry as you the buyer can look at lots (or ALL) the houses for sale in your target market, right from your PC or mobile device.

This is very convenient and low cost, but you still need to go look in person before you buy.

The big online resources are Realtor.com, Zillow.com, Redfin.com, Trulia.com, ETC.

Every Real Estate company and every agency has a website and/or a web presence.

Many realtors also sponsor their own personal web efforts from mailing lists, text lists, websites, Facebook accounts, brochures, pay per click ads, Facebook pages, etc., etc. The options are vast and many.

Real Estate is one of the highest dollar industries in the world, so a lot of effort and money goes into advertising.

So, how do you break it down and sort it out?

All licensed Realtors belong to the Multiple Listing Service. It's the industry's core organization, usually referred to as the MLS.

The MLS owns Realtor.com. All realtors list their for-sale properties on the MLS, and that means they are on Realtor.com

Realtor dot com is the site you want to set up searches with.

EVERY house for sale is listed on the MLS website aka Realtor.com

Realtors work a specific area; you should be considering a wide area of choices.

THIS PART IS IMPORTANT, VERY IMPORTANT. Again, you ideally want to work with the listing realtor, for the reasons I share in this document, so avoid signing any relationship agreements with any realtor, they limit your options.

Realtors will want you to sign an agreement before they start shopping for you, i.e., Look at realtor dot com…. So why not just look yourself? You do not want to get married to one realtor; you want to keep all your options open.

Almost every house listed on the MLS's Realtor.com has interior and exterior photos as well as a "Virtual" tour where on your smartphone, tablet or desktop you can virtually walk through the house as if you are there.

These virtual tours are really good, the industry has good technology to help you find your new home.

Take the few minutes to do the virtual tour, this may save you days of house hunting as you may find what you want faster, or eliminate some sooner.

Time is of the essence as in today's world houses tend to sell FAST! At least, the good ones do!

Online services that attempt to determine property valuations are well known to be inaccurate as they predominately focus on size of the house and often do not accurately take into consideration the location.

They also do not see the view or other highly influencing features of many properties. If you are dealing with a custom home, a rural location, or anything unique the valuation may be way off on one of these websites.

For this and other reasons, lenders still use a real live appraiser.

Professional licensed realtors don't much like online services that provide swag valuations, without a site visit.

Another reason online websites with "estimates" of a home's value are often WAY WRONG is they only calculate off nearby sales using square feet, not comparable properties.

For example, if a block from you a dump of a foreclosure home sells at deep discount due to its condition, these online websites estimate your value using that totally non-comparable house as a comparable, when in fact no appraiser alive would consider it a comparable.

Online valuation algorithms don't take into account many of a home's features, like views, hearing street noise or lack of street noise, hearing the quiet solitude, etc.

The more custom, rural, expensive or unique an area is, the worse online valuation algorithms estimates become.

Online non-MLS websites often copy photos from unknown sources, they post maps showing lot lines that are taken from county assessors tax maps that are inaccurate, not accurate legal surveys.

I have never owned a property where any online real estate system got the price estimate or the property boundaries correct.

MOST of the surveyors' boundaries for my properties vs. what shows on a tax map-based website with lot lines are 10 to 30 feet off minimum, that is significantly incorrect.

The online valuation vs. a real appraisal have never been correct either for any property I have bought or sold.

A county assessor's tax map looks like a map of lot lines, might look to a novice like a survey map, but they all say right on every page "Lot lines approximated for tax collection only and are not survey maps" – yet these online services present the lot line maps to you like they are survey maps – they are very approximate.

If there is a survey on file for a specific property, you can find it at the county's surveyor office as part of the public record, meaning you can access it for free.

Most county surveyors' offices charge a fee to get printed copies. Many counties now have survey maps online available via your county's website.

I always want to know pretty exactly where the property lines are when I buy a property, so I take a few minutes and find the survey map that covers the parcel.

However, surveys are not "proof of ownership", they are, as my attorney once told me, "Evidence of Ownership".

If push really comes to shove and competing property owners end up in court, then a Judge in a court of law decides where property lines are, not the surveyors, often though taking into account the surveys in making their ruling.

Most online real estate websites also allow self-sellers to list; they do not verify info. You want to avoid a for-sale by owner.

Also known as a "FSBO" "For Sale By Owner" (pronounced "fizz-bo")

The process of selling and buying is a legal one. It is a huge investment and it needs to be done correctly to protect your money.

Buying a house from a guy you meet online is like hiring a brain surgeon in a bar.

You should want a licensed realtor as they are educated, licensed and have insurance Licensed realtors will follow the law.

Agents all have Brokers (their boss per se) who owns the agency. Brokers have much more experience, knowledge and provide guidance to their agents to further help them follow the law.

Brokers make a very nice living, they will not compromise their livelihood on any illegitimate deal, they review every deal their agents do and they will stop a deal if it's going to likely get them in a bad situation, they are pretty honest people in my experience.

Licensed Realtors know how to deal with many situations that come up during the course of buying or selling a property. You never know what you will run into.

We had a realtor on one of our properties, some land, who showed it to a buyer. The guy liked the property and wanted to buy it; in fact, he states he will pay full price.

The guy goes over to his vehicle, gets out a duffle bag, walks over to our realtor, drops it at his feet and says, "there's half the money, I can stop by your office tomorrow with the rest".

Our realtor, a true professional, looked down and noted the bag was zipped closed.

He told the guy, "I don't know what's in the bag, but I think I do, and I'm not even touching it, that's not how this works. If you cannot wire the funds through to escrow, we cannot accept them. We don't do dirty cash green money sales."

The guy was a bit surprised, but obviously he's got hundreds of thousands of dollars in bags, he's up to some illegal activity, even if it's "just" tax evasion, that's still very illegal, there is no way a professional realtor would get himself or his buyer involved in anything shady or dodgy.

The guy left, with his bag, never to be heard from again.

My point is a professional realtor will keep you out of bad situations. I encourage everyone to go to the state's website before contacting any realtor and check their record.

Your state has a department of real estate that has a simple license lookup that will show you any issues the realtor has had… such as complaints, suspensions, lawsuits, disciplinary actions.

More often than not, it simply shows they are in good standing with a clear, clean record. Most realtors are true professional who care a lot about their reputation.

Summarized, here is one way to find a house to buy –

1) Decide where you want to buy,

2) Find out what you can afford by getting pre-qualified,

3) Set up a Realtor.com account (free) and;

4) Define a search on realtor.com that will alert you.

5) Stay diligent, look at every alert,

6) Review every property that is in your target area

7) View the virtual tour, if you are still interested do a drive by to look at the location and the surroundings.

8) If still interested, set up a showing with the listing realtor, ASAP!

What to look at when touring a home?

First, you hopefully have the listing agent showing you the house, in my experiences he/she is your conduit to the owner. Be positive, pleasant and complimentary. Sell yourself a bit as well as view the house.

People buy houses, people sell houses – people like people that are likable, it helps to be a likable person.

Remember you will have time to dig deeply into any part of the house AFTER your offer is accepted during the INSPECTION period, during the walkthrough focus on the things you want in a house.

If you never get your offer accepted, then the rest doesn't matter. In my experience, the listing agent, being closest to the sellers, can help you with this, IF they want to.

Don't focus on the décor or the minor cosmetic issues you might encounter. Do remember the must-haves you determined earlier.

Focus on the location.

Try to think long-term.

Try to not get distracted by the current occupant's décor or furnishings.

74

Try to keep emotion out of your review.

Picture yourself in the house. If commuting, think about that. If it needs lots of work, figure out if your budget can handle that.

Try to be positive, view the whole house, walk the outside, review the yard, then go back through the house again. Try not to get fixated on one item.

People who critique something too deeply will sound like a problem to the realtor. The realtor wants to find the right buyers for the seller.

As the old saying goes, you always fight your battles going out the door, not on the way in.

When a seller's agent presents an offer, and they legally have to present all offers unless one has already been accepted, the seller usually says something like "ok, tell me about this buyer"

Realtors will share their opinions, but I have never heard any realtor refer to anyone racially, or any other discriminatory type description. They stick to business, and offer you guidance.

They will certainly say "these are really nice people, might be first time buyers, seem really prepared and ready"

I have also heard a realtor say, "This guy is a real piece of work, he was complaining about everything then he makes this low-ball offer, I think he's going to be a problem if you accept his offer."

Take some time to be cordial to the realtors.

In today's market, people who somehow think they should get a discount just because they are alive, do not understand everyone has a bank full of money and it's a seller's market.

When we sold our third house, we had many, many offers.

We actually put that house in escrow 9 times, it's very common for an escrow to fall out. On that house we had really bad luck, but plenty (like 50! backup offers.)

One buyer took ill and dropped out – hard to think about a new house when you just learned you have cancer, another woman did not see the house until after it was in escrow, and she hated it – everything about it and dropped out.

One couple opened escrow, and 2 weeks later decided to get divorced vs. buy a home. Another buyer lied so badly on his "no doc' loan his lender dropped him, another buyer was contingent upon the sale of

76

their house and it fell out of escrow so there went their money.

We finally got it sold, it's a process, an uncertain process that plays out to an end.

Be prepared before you go look at a house in person quickly when you see one online that piques your interest!

This will save you a lot of time, money and possible discouragement.

You can cover a lot more "ground", by looking at more homes faster by using the online tools, photos, virtual tours, tax reports, etc. that the listing agent has posted on realtor.com

When you look at homes online, you will get a sense what you do or do not want, without the delay and expense of travel.

If you are buying this with a partner or spouse, sit down together, look, discuss, enjoy the comradery of finding out what is important to both of you.

I recently spoke to a married couple about finding a home to buy, the wife was adamant it had to be "very near the husband's work, she did not want him driving a long way every day".

However, his thought was "up to an hour commute is OK if it helps us get what we want".

They were not on the same page at all simply because they had not thought about or discussed it at all! And the amount of commute for many people is basic.

That old cliché is very often true, "If you fail to prepare, then you prepare to fail."

Before you look seriously at a house, you should think through your must-have items.

I suggest you build yourself a written list of "must-haves" to help yourself focus on what you want. If buying with a partner, make it a joint list that you both agree with completely.

You may want to add in a few "nice to haves", items that you would like to have, or would like to be able to add later after buying the house.

I try to keep my list to less than the top ten items that I want in a home.

Build your written list and take that list with you when you do your first walk through, you might find this helpful to stay focused.

I personally always take a notepad or use my PDA to make notes when doing a walk through a home.

I pop photos with my smart phone too, always after asking the realtor if it's OK, some people get weird about strangers taking photos inside their home, I don't blame them.

Items that most likely are important are - Location, price range, size, key features –

For instance, my must-have list might look like this.

Location 30 miles or less from work

$700 – 800k price range

1600 – 2400 sq feet

At least 2 bedrooms and 2 bathrooms

Good sized kitchen (I cook!)

No stairs, one level

Some kind of interesting view

Room to park a motorhome (and needs to be legal in that neighborhood)

No Pool – must have big garage

So that might be my list – Yours might well be very different - I suggest keep it to 10 items, with 1 to 3 being Location, price and size.

A couple years ago my wife and I saw a house that was of interest to us.

It was big, about 5000 sq feet, with view, and listed for only $500k! That's dirt cheap at $100. per sq foot and I wanted to know why it was so cheap.

The online photos looked great, we kind of knew the area was good too.

It was a 3 story with a kitchen on level 2 and level 3. It even had an elevator, all very modern construction.

I contacted the listing agent and set up a meet for the next afternoon.

Next morning at about 9am, my phone rings and it's the listing agent. He tells me he is sorry but he cannot show us the house today.

I ask him why, and he tells me the owner was in hospice and they just took her to the hospital, her son says she most likely will not make it through the day.

WOW!

He promises to keep me posted, but ethically he cannot show the house under these conditions, not to mention if she did die, it would be a waste of his and our time.

3 days later, he calls me and asks if we are still interested in seeing the house.

YES, we can drive right up, be there in an hour. He says OK, meet you at 1 PM at the house.

We drive up, curious as to what happened to the owner so we chat about that in the driveway when we get there.

Now, this is an example of the value of working with the listing agent, no other agent would have this insight. He shares she recovered enough to go back to hospice, and he had spoken with her on the phone, she seemed mentally competent to him and she instructed him to continue to find a buyer.

At this point, I am getting the impression this is some kind of urgent matter, so I share with him we would be cash buyers if we like it, but I also ask why the big rush and what's to say she does not expire before escrow closes?

He shares she lives out of state, they could do a fast escrow at our discretion.

The seller desperately wants to sell the house so the funds move into her trust as cash, she wants the house converted to cash because she knows her heirs will fight over the house – Cash is just divided.

The seller is trying to avoid a family fight after her death, and that will help her rest in peace.

He says he can't guarantee she will last until close of escrow – Understandable.

We did the site visit, met the listing agent, also the broker of his firm, and reviewed the house.

81

It took a quite a while, a couple hours.

It was more like a hotel than a home, room after room, large sitting rooms, bedrooms all with 12-foot ceilings with great crown molding impeccably painted.

There was an 8-car garage on the ground floor, elevator and lots of bonus areas on the first floor as unfinished space.

It all looked brand new. There was even an attached RV garage that was 80 x 40 with 4 10 foot wide 16-foot-high doors.

The 2 kitchens had beautiful stone that matched the 5 bathrooms. All faucets were gold-plated faucets, gorgeous porcelain tile, real hardwood and lush carpet – everything looked brand new and then the entire yard around the house was road base, like a huge parking lot? Odd.

I got the sense the previous owners might have been in trucking, RV, fishing, construction or some other kind of business that involved a need to park a lot of big vehicles. It was quite interesting.

The property was zoned R-4, I thought about buying it and making it into 2 condos or a duplex, or even 4 units – it was that big!

But it was so huge, just a whole lot of everything.

We really did not have the time for another project, but it was SO value-priced. I figured most likely a low-ball offer might be accepted.

My experience taught me maybe I should have a chat with my attorney about a death-bed out of state sale…. His advice was simple – don't get involved.

We had already concluded it was just too big to live in for us, it would have been a project, and not really something we had time for.

Sometimes a deal is just too good to be true, I don't believe in taking advantage of people, and this just did not feel right.

We walked away. My point is, you should know what you want, and be prepared to walk away and we got much more insight to the seller's motivation and her frame of mind by working with the listing agent.

Questions I ask during the showing

I take my written list to try to keep myself focused – I Add notes other items I see during the showing as we walk through

83

1)   I re-read the listing before the showing – I often print it out and highlight anything I want to ask about. If it has a virtual tour, I take the virtual tour and make any notes of things I want to know more about or see in person.

2)   I ask the realtor if they think the house will appraise for the listing price?

3)   I ask How big is this house? – in square feet

4)   Does the house belong to an HOA and if yes, what are the fees?

HOA is Home Owners Association, there are usually monthly fees from a couple hundred to a couple thousand – there may be other benefits and costs, if there is an HOA get all the information about it from your realtor.

5)   Building Permits - If the house looks home-made, added on to, or has a bonus room in the backyard, ask about permits. If there was a permit, they will know it and have copy, if not they will evade – and you can check into it later if interested in the property by visiting the county building department.

6)   Are the property boundaries marked?

7)   Easements – Does anyone other than utilities have an easement across any part of the property?

8)   I verify the age of the home. If older, when was it remodeled? Ask the realtor, or lift up the toilet tank lid, on the inside of the toilet tank lid is a date of manufacture – very few people change the toilet.

9)   I look for upgrades. Are there any known defects (read declarations before offer)?

10) Are the appliances included?

11) What is the heat source?

Electric? Gas? Oil?

12) Does the neighborhood have CC&R's?

VERY IMPORTANT – CC&R's

Covenants, Conditions and Restrictions (CC&Rs) are rules and property limitations of a planned community neighborhood. Perhaps you have a travel trailer and want to park it in your driveway. Many communities have local zoning, ordinances or covenants in the CCR's that prohibit parking an RV on the street or in your yard or driveway.

13) What are the schools like? If you have, or are planning to have school age children, this is an important concern. Do a drive-by, check out

the school online, call the office and see if you can come visit. Your realtor may have an opinion here too.

14)   Go with an open-ended, non-specific question designed to encourage more conversation like "Tell me about the house?"

15)   Are there any contingencies from the sellers?

Contingencies are clauses in the contract between seller and buyer that define a condition or action that must be met for the contract to become binding.

The contingency becomes part of a binding sales contract when both parties, the buyer and the seller, agree to the terms and sign the contract.

It is important to understand what contingency clauses are included in your real estate contract – again I stress read the contract before you sign, go over it with your realtor, have your attorney review it and if you do not understand, don't sign.

There are somewhat "custom and ordinary contingencies" like the deal is contingent upon all inspections being completed by the buyer, the buyer's loan is approved, the appraisal finds the

86

right value, the seller's new house deal closes, the buyer's old house closes…. things like that.

There can be weird things that sellers or buyers might ask the deal to be contingent on. I try to stay openminded in this area until I fully understand the ask that the contingency creates.

Things like the buyers' job transfer comes through, the seller's son gets paroled, etc.

Contingent clauses can be just about anything, so ask before you offer, does the seller have any contingencies?

If you can avoid including a weird contingency request in your offer, that might help your offer be accepted.

For instance, let's say you like the sofa in the living room, you can ask that to be included in the sale… but that might be a big problem for the seller if, say it's an antique from their great-grandmother's house.

However, in this type situation talk to the realtor, the seller might be happy to leave that big old ugly couch vs. paying movers to carry it out! You never know what someone's perspective is until you politely ask!

What NOT to do when touring a home

It's important to maintain a positive outlook when touring a home.

The property may not be what you want, you may see this immediately, but still give it a good look through.

The realtor has taken their time to show you the house, give it a good look through so as not to insult the realtor. Thank them for their time.

It's funny but sometimes after you look at a home, you're really sure it's not the one. But later after looking at others, thinking about the property, it just might be offer-worthy after all.

Try to look past the current occupants' furnishings and décor. I never ever comment negatively on anything inside the house – If you have the listing agent showing the house, chances are they are friends of the seller, because ALL realtors are your friends when they are going to make a commission off you.

Remember, realtors are salespeople trying to do their job and that job is to sell something to someone like you.

You do not want to paint yourself as negative, critical or skeptical. If you don't like the house, don't buy it.

Trash talking a property will not bring the price down, it just annoys people.

If you feel it's worth less than they are asking, and you seriously are interested, you can cover this issue with the realtor when the two of you write the offer.

Hopefully you have developed, as I suggested, a list of things you want in a home, as well as things you do not want. Don't forget what is on your list.

Don't use the bathroom, or bounce on the bed. Don't open cabinets, or doors without asking the realtor permission.

If there are locked areas, ask what's in there and move on, if you offer on the house, you can ask these areas be opened up before submitting.

We bought a house the previous owners were using as a vacation rental and as their vacation home and their RV storage location.

When we toured the home, the 3 rooms downstairs were locked up, the listing agent realtor did not even have a key.

We were told the sellers are using this for vacation rental, their personal items are stored in there.

OK, that made sense.

We liked the house, we wanted to offer, we simply asked the realtor to find out if we could view the downstairs rooms, the owner met us and unlocked them, apparently, he did not trust his realtor, and that's OK!

Sellers often lock a room with their valuables inside. Maybe the owner has a large gun safe in the den or a collection of something valuable that they do not want everyone to see, it's common. Just ask to see inside if you are interested in making an offer on the property.

If you run into the owner when touring the home, thank them for allowing you into their home. Do not engage in any discussion that could be perceived as biased or negative.

IF you decide to make an offer and if it's accepted, you will have an inspection period during which you or your inspector(s) can open everything with the seller's realtor present, so don't over-explore.

Don't not ask a question. You may not get an answer, or you may get an, "I'll ask the owner and get back to you" type answer.

Phraseology is a bit important; discretion is always the better part of valor. For instance, let's say there is a bonus room, and you want to know it there was a building permit.

If there is no permit, the appraiser will not count the space as GLA, and may even note to the lender there is an unpermitted addition… but when you are doing a walkthrough and you're wondering, simply ask if the owner has a copy of the permit. The add-on may have been done by a previous owner, they may or may not even know if it was permitted.

If no copies of any permits are provided by seller, your easy option is to ask the realtor to check with the building department, they will know where to go and will get the info right away.

Building permits are usually public record, readily available for walk-in review.

I never ever say something like, "if there is no permit, I want a discount".

Again, I deal with any issues in the offer stage of the purchase with your realtor's guidance.

Everyone's role in a real estate sale

Job of a Realtor

Realtors are sales people – it may appear to you they do very little work, but that is not the case, they do a lot of work behind the scenes as they work to earn their commission.

Realtors are well-compensated from a sale.

You DO NOT want to get married to any one realtor, DO NOT sign an exclusivity agreement or any such document with any realtor. The only document you sign is an offer when you make one.

Be pleasant, but remember a realtor is not your attorney, everything you tell them is something they may share, repeat or use as they want – there is no confidentiality.

Your realtor is not your mom, they typically will not comment on things unless you ask.

Answers are usually vague and deflective. For instance, say you express concern about the roof – Your realtor is not a licensed roofer, so they will say – we can ask for a roof report.

If you write your offer, and state "We want a roof report from a licensed roofer at the seller's expense", the seller might then say …. "Next". And your offer is allowed to lapse, expire, get rejected, etc.

The correct way to handle any concerns is in the INSPECTION PHASE, not the offer phase. You will have usually 17 days to bring in inspectors.

Yes, YOU WILL PAY these inspectors, but they will provide an honest opinion. IF you list out what inspections you want the seller to pay for, they might simply take the next offer that does not seem so onerous and costly, so I think carefully before I ask for the sellers to pay for anything.

Your realtor wants you to buy a house, that's how they make a living. They want you to buy the most house you can afford, that's how they make a living.

Your realtor will not kill any sale intentionally by bring forward defects…. they are not really qualified or licensed to comment on most things structural and such.

Realtors are prohibited from commenting on "good vs. bad" neighborhoods. In today's world they all have been educated to avoid anything that could be perceived as racial, defamatory, judgmental or anything that will get them in trouble.

Your realtor is a professional salesperson, that's how they make their living.

Trust but verify everything everyone says, including your own realtor, after all at the end of the day, you have to live with the purchase, any defects and all those monthly payments.

Anything a realtor "tells" you, is superseded by the written documentation you will sign or receive, so read what you sign.

Sleep on all documents, ask questions but if it's not in writing, it does not exist.

Home buying is a business deal. Nothing in the sale is going to cost the realtor anything, they will forget to mention anything that might kill their sale.

Realtors are not (usually unless they also have a contractor's license or some such thing) not qualified nor licensed to comment on most things, like plumbing, electrical, roofing, permitting, etc.- they might comment, but they are making un-qualified comments.

Your realtor is most likely not your friend, they are sales people so they are charming and

94

pleasant. After the sale, your realtor is your ex-realtor… and we all know how it can be with ex's.

Just remember, you as buyer will ultimately pay for everything. If you do not understand something, stop, ask questions and hire expert licensed advice. Always be prepared to walk away from a deal.

You can infer a lot of knowledge from a realtor during walk-through. I prefer to use the listing agent as I have found lots of insight and knowledge that any other agent simply would not have since they do not know the owners.

I once looked at a property with the listing agent, and in the idle conversation that occurs during a walk through, she commented that she had sold the house to the current owners 25 years ago.

The property was just listed, I think I was the first to see it. I asked the realtor how the asking price was determined, she stated the sellers came up with the price, and she shared she thought it was low.

That clued her to mention, by the way, the sellers indicated they are not making any changes, repairs, paying for any inspections or making any warranties about the house, they just want out – it's being sold "As Is!"

95

As we entered the master suite and master bathroom, she says, "this is exactly the same house I sold them, this is the same carpet from 25 years ago, nothing has changed."

I inferred from this idle conversation that perhaps something went wrong in the seller's life – no changes, no repairs, maybe they just want / need out?

I bought the house, at their asking price, paid cash and entered into a 15-day escrow.

During the escrow process I learned they had a mortgage that was just about asking price plus realtor commission, indeed they literally just wanted out.

After about $50k of additional investment to refresh the interior, the house doubled in value.

The ex-owners were very happy to move on, and I to move in!

Job of Escrow Officer

The escrow Officer does the most work in any deal, she knows all the law and organizes the entire escrow exactly as the law prescribes.

Escrow officers work for title companies, and despite the fact they are paid by sellers and/or buyers, they do not do anything that is shady or in favor of one party vs. the other.

Escrow Officers have a fiduciary duty to all parties to correctly and legally do their duties.

Escrow Officers are very busy people and very efficient as they live in a world of deadlines and commitments.

Escrow officers are well compensated, and are usually very professional.

The escrow officer is like a wedding planner, they make sure everything goes correctly and have a lot of experience to get the job done right.

The escrow officer is NOT your attorney! If you have legal questions about anything you do not understand, invest an hour with your attorney or find one that specializes in REAL ESTATE in the area you are buying in.

If you do not comply with providing what your escrow officer asks you to provide in a very timely manner (Right NOW Quickly please!) then you risk having your deal canceled.

The escrow officer always needs your attention immediately. They are usually very helpful nice people, but they are also very busy. Most try to do almost everything by e-mail or DocuSign, so keep an eye on your email.

Job of Loan Officer

Your loan officer guides you through the documentation process – Loan Officers are also for all intrinsic purposes, sales people –

MODERN loan companies do almost everything online, your loan officer is the person who sets this all up, monitors it, answers any questions, raises issues, and is your communication conduit between underwriting, who approves your loan, and yourself.

Job of the Loan Originating Company

Your loan officer works for a company that originates loans. In essence they work with you to collect all the information needed to submit your loan application to "Underwriting".

Underwriting means that your lender verifies your income, assets, debt and property details in order to issue final approval for your loan.

An underwriter is a financial expert who reviews your finances and determines how much risk there is if they decide to give you a loan.

After Underwriting is satisfied, your loan is funded, the deal closes, and typically the loan originating company will submit your loan to be sold.

The Originating Lender usually keeps the first mortgage payment, as it's almost all interest on their money for one month, i.e., the most lucrative payment for the lender.

Fannie Mae and Freddie Mac buy mortgages from lenders and either hold these mortgages in their portfolios or package the loans into mortgage-backed securities (MBS) that are sold on the open market (Wall Street). Lenders use the funds raised by selling mortgages they originated to engage in further lending.

Job of Buyer

YES, you will have a lot to do in a very short time frame. You will need to provide whatever documentation is requested by the loan officer and escrow. The buyer's job is to make decisions as well.

Be honest and forthright, do not guess numbers – look them up - BE AS ACCURATE AS POSSIBLE. do not misspeak or misstate, do not rush signing.

Read everything and ask questions before signing anything.

UNDERSTAND everything before signing. If you do not understand something, find someone – your realtor, your attorney, your CPA to explain it to you until you are comfortable you do understand what you are signing and obligating to.

Running all deals past your attorney is not a bad idea as you pay your attorney by the hour, not the deal.

Once the legal process starts with you submitting an offer, you will be given time limits, mostly timed in days… but the sooner you reply the easier it is.

Escrow will have a big "getting-to-know-you" questionnaire so the escrow agent can get you the right documentation.

Almost all signing is online DocuSign type attestations, except the close, that's done in person.

A little bit about DIY

I'd be remiss if I did not take a moment here to talk a little bit about DIY…. DIY = "do it yourself" building and repairs.

MANY people want a house with some rough edges, some challenging things they can DIY and resolve.

DIY projects take 2-3 times longer than you think, and cost 3-4 times more than you want to spend.

I always TRY really hard to buy something I am happy with day one, despite all the potential I might see, that's for the future… maybe in a few years I can add that gym level above the garage, this is my approach.

IF you DIY, make sure you pull the proper permits. SO many of the TV shows never cover that aspect of renovating.

Permits are quite often over-the-counter and not that expensive. OR they can require engineering that gets very costly in a hurry.

I have many times stopped by the building department before making an offer. They usually can tell you a lot about the house and a lot about if they will approve your DIY ideas, BEFORE you buy.

Job of Seller

To work with their realtor and make the property available for viewing, inspecting, appraising, etc. To answer questions quickly and accurately.

Another job of the Sellers is to honestly disclose a litany of things about the property that may or may not influence your decision to buy.

This is done via the written disclosures, a multiple page form of standardized questions and answers, usually as "Yes, No, Don't Know"

You will usually receive the disclosures after your offer accepted, they often do reveal some personal information so they are provided after the offer is accepted as this way not every looky loo gets the intel.

You will have 17 days after the offer accepted to review the disclosures, and ask further questions, drop the deal, or at least base your inspections on some of the answers provided.

Disclosures can be extensive, and are usually good information.

For instance, if the disclosures tell me that the house is on septic vs. city sewer, then I know I need to get a septic engineer out to pump out and then inspect the tank and leach field system.

If the disclosures tell me the owner does not know how old the roof is, then I will get a roofer to inspect the roof.

Ask your realtor about anything you see that needs to be clarified for your understanding.

I bought a property once, a very nice but older home, and the realtor shared with me that we should get a sewer hookup inspection. This was a new one to me, but the realtor explained that the house was built before the city's sewer system, and way back then you had to pay to get hooked up.

Way back then, some homeowners just kept their old septic tank and paid the mandatory monthly sewer fee.

The hookup test was simple and free.

My realtor contacted the city's public works department and they sent a guy out who flushed a UV dye pack down a toilet. He then opened the sewer manhole in the street and shined in a ultra-violet light down the hole into the public sewer.

We all watched the blue dyed water flow by confirming that, yes, the house was on sewer, and the deal went forward.

If the disclosures are not completed by the sellers, or are missing some or many of the answers to the standard questions ask, you can your realtor to ask for them to be complete.

Disclosures are several pages of questions about the property, Things like "does the roof leak?'

Yes, no, don't know are the answer options.

Seller says no, you move in, roof leaks, you now have grounds for a lawsuit.

Most sellers try to be as accurate as possible. If they say "don't know" on the roof leaking, that's when I get a roof report by a professional reputable roofer (and you the buyer pays for these extra inspections.

You can ask the seller to pay for additional inspections, but in this sellers' market, usually that won't happen – the seller will just go to the next buyer.

You want to look carefully at the disclosure statement. Items marked "Don't Know" are something you will want to follow up on. Again, ask questions until you are satisfied you understand what you are buying.

Disclosures are provided to buyers after the offer is accepted as part of the inspection period.

If something is disclosed that is untenable to you, you can usually cancel the deal and usually get your deposit back. Ask your realtor to confirm this as it falls in the category of "local rules" regarding deposits and refunds of deposits **BEFORE** you hand them your deposit funds.

Deposit as LITTLE as needed.... DON'T deposit $50,000 when $1,000. Will do the job. Ask your realtor.

Most Realtors will guide sellers to say Don't know if there is any doubt of their knowledge on a specific subject covered by the disclosures.

I made an offer on a house one time that was accepted and then when the preliminary title report arrived, it showed an easement across the entire property but the sellers' disclosures stated "no Easements"

We canceled the deal as this type of easement was untenable.

It's typical and ordinary for utility companies to have easements, but not over the entire property including the house!

Home Buying Process - High Level

Usually, In this order –

1. Review your finances
2. Review Your Credit Reports
3. Save money for down payment, closing & moving.
4. Get pre-approved for a loan
5. Shop for a home
6. Get an offer to buy accepted by a seller
7. Open Escrow
8. Get the property appraised
9. Inspect the property
10. Do all the paperwork as needed
11. Close the loan and close escrow
12. Move in!

Gosh, that sounds easy, but it takes a lot of time and due diligence to get it done.

Remember, sometimes things simply do not work out, no matter how much you try, work or wish something will happen, it sometimes is just not meant to be.

Personally, that's when I start over and try again. Quite often the journey is as interesting as the destination. I try to enjoy the journey.

Loan Types

ALMOST all mortgages are backed by the federal government, regardless of who originates them. In 1934 Congress created the 2 home mortgage lending giants FreddyMac and FannieMae.

These 2 quasi-governmental agencies buy almost all mortgages, package them into mortgage-backed securities and sell them to the investor community with guarantees of payment.

This is all done to keep mortgage rates low, assure payments are made and stabilize the American dream of home ownership.

This means Freddy and Fannie have basically set the rules for ALL aspects of the mortgage industry and almost all of the home buying process – since they control the money.

Your Loan documents will comply to their standards and your loan officer at the loan originating company (bank, mortgage bank, etc.) will use their software to comply.

I just greatly summarized what Freddy and Fannie do, if you want super detail, giggle it with your favorite web browser.

There are intense political views on Freddy and Fannie, me, I don't get political, I just want a loan to buy a house.

VA loans
(Veterans Administration Loan Programs)

VA loans are available for honorably discharged veterans and they have a lower annual percentage rate than conventional loans.

They also have programs that require a much smaller percentage of a down payment!

The VA loan has "approved" and "Non approved" items, meaning you cannot put some things into the mortgage like you can in a conventional loan.

Lenders are limited what the VA will pay in fees, so the lenders charge the buyers separately.

VA loans have a reputation of slow to fund, and everything in the house is tested and must work perfectly OR the SELLER must pay to fix before close.

Many sellers won't get near a VA loan as it can cost them money untold. Sellers and sellers' realtors will not say this out loud, but there is some headwinds to be found when using a VA loan.

It also precludes you buying a fixer as most true fixers have lots of stuff that is not functioning.

A house being purchased with a VA loan MUST have all the appliances provided by the seller, and be in perfect working order. VA Appraisals are usually twice as expensive as conventional.

It's a good program for veterans to save money buying a home, just be prepared for some delay.

Conventional Loan

The standard conventional 80/20 loan. 20% down payment, 80% loan…. up to $647,200. (2022 limits). These limits are adjusted annually by the federal government.

You usually can tuck some of the closing costs into a conventional loan.

Conventional loans can have larger down payments – Like 50% down, 50% financed, or any other percentage above 20% down, and this lowers your payments obviously. The more you put in, the less you finance.

JUMBO Loan

Any loan over $647,200. (The 2022 FHA determined top limit for a conventional loan, is considered a Jumbo

Jumbo loans carry a slightly higher interest rate, meaning you pay more for the risk the lender assumes as Freddy and Fannie don't buy Jumbos.

Often, your lender will guide you, if possible, to save you money, to a conventional first mortgage, and a second mortgage vs. a Jumbo to reduce your cost as Jumbos typically have higher interest rates.

This can be especially beneficial if you have the means to pay down the second in a few years thereby eliminating a portion of the monthly payment.

I had a Jumbo loan about 20 years ago, I nick-named my Jumbo mortgage Dumbo…. LOL

110

PMI

If your Loan to value ratio is not 80/20… meaning your down payment is only 15%, then they do sell "Payment Mortgage Insurance" per month. It's VERY expensive and you really want to avoid.

Impounds

"Impounds" is the name of the process wherein your loan servicer, the people you make your mortgage payable to, collects as part of the monthly loan payment a twelfth of your annual property tax funds and annual property insurance funds.

The loan servicer holds your monies in an escrow account and then pays your property taxes and property insurance from these funds when they are due. Most mortgages have impounds, not a bad thing.

PITI

P.I.T.I. = simply is an abbreviation for "principal, interest, taxes and insurance" In essence your entire mortgage payment with Impounds.

"Owner Will Carry"

"Owner carries paper", "Owner financing" – all these mean the previous owner finances your purchase, you make your payments to the old owner.

Although it appears to eliminate a lot of the loan work, it's a very dangerous deal. This is NOTHING you should get involved with.

Owners carry when the house will not appraise, or it has issues that prevent it from getting real financing – like no permit.

When a lender pulls the history on a home, and it reads 1 bedroom one bath and the house now has 3 bathrooms and 5 bedrooms, they will not make a loan – it's got permit issues.

When you apply for Homeowners insurance, the insurance companies all use a common database that tells them about the subject property.

If you are buying a 4 bedroom 3 bathroom home, and the database says it's a 1 bathroom 2 bedroom, they will not insure you, and the deal is dead.

I made an offer that was accepted by the sellers of a home a number of years ago. When I called my insurance agent to obtain homeowners insurance, I had an interesting experience.

My broker works for a large national well know reputable insurance company, whose name I'll omit from this story. When my broker entered the houses address, it came up as a 96-year-old house with 228 square feet – But the house I was buying was ~1600 square feet!

Someone forgot to get permits a long time ago!

That deal then died a I did not want to buy a problem. I also learned to check the insurability of the house before the inspection period ends!

My view always has been, If I cannot qualify for a mortgage on a property, due to the condition of the property, then I don't want it as I'd be buying someone else's problem property.

No one wants to own a problem property.

I avoid "owner will Carry" due to the many complexities it creates for the buyer (me).

For instance, in California, when an owner carries paper, the BUYER must file a 1099 tax document to the IRS and the State EACH AND EVERY YEAR for the entire life of the mortgage, detailing to the California State Tax Board about the payments made to the seller (aka Mortgage Holder).

The BUYER also has to withhold a portion of the payment using the State Franchise Tax Board rules, submit that withholding each month to the IRS and the State. – If the BUYER does not do this per state and federal regulations, the buyer is additionally responsible for the SELLERS taxes being paid.

Massive work, big liability, etc. I never get involved in "Owner Will Carry".

Second Mortgage

Sometimes it makes financial sense for people have more than one mortgage on the same property.

When you have 2 or more, mortgages they are referred to as a "First Mortgage" and a "Second Mortgage" also often abbreviated to the words First and Second.

The lender who is in First place (AKA the first mortgage) has vastly superior legal rights if the buyer defaults – i.e. Can't pay, won't pay or are unavailable to pay (like maybe they died)

Typically, any second mortgages are priced more like a hard money loan, secured by the property, but at much higher interest rates.

Sometimes people will do a conventional and a second to avoid JUMBO interest rates. A loan officer will guide you; they always want to help you borrow – They too are sales people.

IF there are 2 mortgages, a first and second, and the property loses value and is sold for less than owed, the First gets paid FIRST, the second gets what is left over, if any

IF you don't pay your mortgage, for whatever reason, the lender forecloses, a very lengthy process, and then they seize the property. Not good to not pay.

If you ever find yourself in a position where you cannot pay, it's best to contact the lender and talk with them. Maybe they have some idea's, maybe they will do a "work-out" agreement, or give you time to sell the property vs. full foreclosure.

There are some valid reasons for 2 mortgages, one is if you are moving from one owned home to another, say a job transfer but there is not time to sell before buying.

In this case you might do a second mortgage to provide the down payment for the new house, knowing when you sell you will get the funds to pay it off.

This is called "Bridge Financing".

Another reason for a second is to finance something with the equity in your home, but leaving your first mortgage (that might have a great interest rate) intact.

The very popular HELOC - "Home Equity Line of Credit" is technically a second (or third) mortgage, secured by the home, but it acts like a line of credit it can be extended or overpaid at the borrower's discretion.

HELOC's interest paid is often tax deductible.

Some homeowners finance their auto purchases via their HELOC vs. an auto loan.

Often a lower interest rate, but tax deductible. All this requires careful thought, and sometimes guidance from a CPA is helpful.

Lease to Own

This is like RTO (Rent To Own) furniture, generally thought to be a bad idea.

If you cannot afford to buy the house today, find one you can afford and/or wait and save more down payment while increasing your income.

Points and Pre-Paid Interest

"Points" is a phrase to describe a loan feature where you prepay interest, and it lowers your rate and payment. This basically means you open a loan, then pre-pay part of it.

The reason people will do this is that money you buy the Points with, is partially or completely deductible... and principal payments are not deductible, only the interest.

I suggest study a mortgage table a bit with some "what-if's" and you most likely will see points don't do much to help a young mortgage, but this is a personal decision that might need to include your tax planning professional.

What is a Full Doc Loan?

You will most likely be doing a full doc loan.

Full Documentation means that you will provide written evidence that substantiates everything you tell your lender and answer every question they ask.

The loan Originator (mortgage company) via the loan officer and their website will give you a detailed list. Then they review, and might ask questions about specific items.

Many people believe the housing crash of 2008 was essentially created by "No Doc' loans.

A no Doc loan is where they loaned people money based upon no documentation, they just trusted what the applicant told them.

Income was not verified, credit scores were not used much, thus the phrase "no

Documentation", they did charge a slightly higher interest rate.

The underlying principle was everyone deserves a mortgage and since real estate always goes up (but it does not), no one could lose money.

So, they just loaned, and loaned and loaned, millions of irresponsible people money to buy a home that many could not afford.

These no doc loans are no longer done this way…. For the obvious reasons.

You can expect at a minimum to provide the following documentation, usually submitted as PDF's if you are using a modern online direct lender as your loan originator.

This will apply for ALL persons on the loan or on the title of the house.

Copy of Federal and State tax returns – ALL pages last 2 years

Copy of ALL W-2's last 3 years

Copy of driver's license,

Last 2 months' current paycheck stubs,

Current Employer info for verification,

All bank statements – time frame can vary,

Last month's statement where your down payment resides in your name.

They will ask about how you obtained the down payment – answers like Salary, Gift, Inheritance, settlement, lottery, Vegas, ETC.

If your down payment is part gift, they may want a letter from the "Giftor" stating it's a gift (and not a loan) and the taxes are paid on it.

If you won your down payment somewhere, like the lottery, Las Vegas or crypto gambling, they most likely will want to see where you accounted for it to the IRS on your tax return and also have some proof you paid the taxes due on the income.

Lenders will have standard Y/N questions, citizenship, years of education, Etc.

Lenders may question your job history if job time less than 2 years, they will ask about things like child support, spousal support, tax issues, etc., anything on your taxes or credit report is fair game for more granular detail.

Lenders will want to know about all forms of income, and specifically that the taxes are paid, they will verify most everything, they will want written copies of agreements, statements, etc. to substantiate everything you tell them.

120

Remember that most often the ultimate lender is backed by the federal government so please be carefully accurate.

Inaccurate answers on a mortgage application can be considered mortgage fraud, so take the time to look up the exact number, don't guess.

You ideally want to work with a DIRECT LENDER, they will have the best pricing… and a mortgage is something you live with a long time so price does matter!

Using a highly convenient modern online mortgage company – I have used several through the years, is really the only way to go. Local mortgage brokers often tuck in additional fees.

I have used a Direct Lender online several times with great ease and success. They give you accurate quotes, you get to see ALL the loan programs, all the options on screen without a salesman pushing you.

When you use an online DIRECT lender, you can see all the options of what happens to payments and principal if you buy points on a loan as every loan is laid out conveniently on screen for your comparison.

You will see on screen how, exactly to the penny, buying points affects the payment. I like to be able to consider different loan options without the salesman pushing one, you know, the one he makes the most money on.

Most Direct Lenders online websites detail every closing cost and many of their loans are "No Fee", saving you money. Most brick-and-mortar brokers add on Fees.

How the loan process works

You will migrate through the following phases – kind of a hoot, but here it is, sometimes lenders add more to it too!

1) Pre-Qualified – This basically means you completed the loan form online.

2) Qualified – This means they got more info from you, it looks good, they have not run your credit or verified you, but they like you.

3) Pre-Approved – this means they ran your credit, verified a couple things, and VERY IMPORTANT HAVE ISSUED YOU A LETTER OF PRE-APPROVAL to attach to your offer to indicate to the seller you're on your way to getting approved for a mortgage.

4) Approved – This means they ask you every question, you answered all, and they are willing to move this to funding if the property all checks out – I.E. Appraisal, inspections and/or title report items.

5) Funded – this is the act of the lender transferring the loaned funds to the escrow officer's account – you are about to close escrow and become a homeowner!

Some Real Estate Terminology

Like many subjects, topics or specialization, real estate has a lot of vertical terminology that only applies to real estate.

You may have heard of some of these phrases, but in case not, here is a list of the more common phrases you will encounter and what they mean in plain English.

Loan to Value (LTV)

Loan to Value   Example if Value = $100,000, a LTV of 80/20 means the down payment is $20,000 and the loan is $80,000

123

Appraisal

This is the process of determining the current market value of the subject property. I covered this extensively in a previous chapter.

Escrow

The honest broker in the middle of the transactions who organizes the entire process of adjudicating all the legally required items to clear, holds and distributes the money, then transfers title from the old owners to the new owners.

When your offer is accepted by the seller, the realtor will then "Open Escrow" with a title company that is mutually agreed upon, usually recommended by your realtor.

The title company assigns one of their employees to be the escrow officer who will do the work of processing the legalities of transferring title from the old owner to the new owner, YOU!

Title companies and Escrow officers are licensed, bonded, highly regulated and process everything to the letter of the law.

Title companies have attorneys on staff, and at the close of escrow they issue title insurance that guarantees the title transfer is OK for the seller's benefit.

Escrow also holds the funds from your lender, and disburses said funds in accordance to escrow instructions the realtors create in writing and both you and the seller mutually agree to by signature.

Again, if you do not understand anything someone is asking you to sign, or agree to, ask questions of your realtor, their broker, the escrow officer, your attorney whoever you need to find and ask BEFORE you sign anything.

Most of it is pretty self-explanatory and easy to follow, but sometimes it gets deep into the legalese.

Closing Escrow means the final days' work the escrow officer does to fund, transfer funds, record the changed title with the county clerk's office where the property resides, and many other things.

You, as buyer, will get a closing escrow statement that details where all your money went for the purchase of the home as well as the closing costs.

Funding

After the loan is approved, as nearly the last part of escrow in the last phase of the escrow, usually on the day of closing or the day before, the transfer of funds from the lender to the escrow agent's account

Closing Costs

Closing Costs are all the fees, paid forward property taxes, transfer taxes, documentation fees, escrow fees, pre-paid points (if any), pre-paid HOA (if any), etc., that you as the buyer will need to pay funds into escrow to in turn pay all these items required to close escrow.

Usually, your lender estimates these when they quote you a loan.

Most online direct lenders detail them out very well as their software has every state and county tax rates built in.

Closing costs are often $10k – $20k OR MORE!

You, the buyer, pays these, usually upfront before escrow closes. SOME closing costs can usually be put into the loan vs cash out of pocket.

Your Loan Originator can detail these for you in an estimate.

It is very important to be prepared to pay your closing costs, if you cannot pay them before escrow closes (when the escrow officer tells you they are due) it can not only mean the end of your deal, but can also have grave legal consequences.

Again, if you do not understand this, talk to your realtor, escrow agent and/or lender early in the escrow.

Property Taxes

The money the property owner pays the county every year. This is usually collected through a process known as "impounds" as part of your monthly mortgage payment.

Property tax in California is usually about 1.1% of the value. Proposition 13 limits the tax rate to 1%, but then they add on local bond issues, school taxes, etc.

Taxes vary state to state, county to county and even city to city. Some states have MUCH higher property tax rates.

Example, you buy a home in California for $800,000., your first-year taxes will be ~8,800. A year, or about $734. A month.

These usually are added onto your mortgage payment in a process called "Impounds" Again, ask your realtor if you have questions.

Property Insurance

Collected the same way, via impounds as part of your monthly payment, however you select the insurance company and plan.

Homeowners insurance can range from $1500 to $3-4,000 a year. The insurance rates are influenced by the location – high fire areas have high insurance.

Flood Certificate

Escrow will order a flood certificate from the people who track flooding.

Using what is known as the 100-year flood model they will determine if the lot your home is on has ever flooded, and what the risk is it will flood again.

Houses that are in flood plains, below flood level, on water's edge, etc. may need "flood Insurance" to close the loan.

Flood insurance is EXTREMELY expensive and only issued by FEMA. If a property is in a flood zone, walk on, it's unaffordable… next!

Preliminary Title Report

After your offer is accepted by the sellers, then Escrow is opened and one of the first tasks the title company via your escrow officer does is pulls from public records the Preliminary Title Report.

The Preliminary Title Report includes all the legal items about the real property, such as who the legal owners are, are there any loans currently secured by the property, taxes paid or past due, judgements, past due child support liens, recorded easements across the property, or any of many other covenants recorded against the property, Etc., Etc.

Your realtor can go over this in detail, it's important you understand what you are buying.

129

Your escrow officer can also explain specific items as she is the one who deals with clearing most of these before transferring into the buyer's name.

Things like recorded easements run with the property, meaning someone has a right to pass over part or all of the property at any time.

In this instance, you will want to see and understand exactly where the easement gives them access and decide if you are OK with this as there is no way to remove an easement once recorded unless all parties agree.

Easements are covenants that run with the property, not the owners.

Re-Fi -

Re-Fi – technically a "Re-Finance of an existing loan" is when you own a home with a mortgage, and you re-finance the loan.

Some valid reasons to do this is to reduce the payment by getting a better interest rate. Maybe your credit score increased, and a better loan is available. Shortening the length of the mortgage can save thousands.

Going from a 30-year loan with 27 years left to a 15-year lower interest higher payment might make sense if your income has increased.

Maybe you inherited some money, so you want to pay down part of your mortgage, unless you re-fi you can make a one-off principal payment and your monthly stays the same.

Say as an example you inherited $50k, and your remaining balance is $310k. By refinancing when you put the $50k into paying down the original mortgage, you may lower your monthly payment.

Talk to your lender when you start thinking about a re-fi. Most lenders are only loan originators, so they are happy to help you originate a re-fi, even if you are paying off a loan that they originally originated for you.

I always shop for a loan; different lenders have different rates. With today's online access, many direct lenders post their DAILY updated mortgage rates.

Google is very helpful in finding Direct lenders, usually you can see their loan packages and rates. They will have a VERY helpful load officer to assist you when you decide to move forward.

Vesting

Vesting is the fancy term for how the title is held – these legal descriptions vary from state to state – your escrow officer will go over this, so ask her to confirm. Further you can confirm with your attorney.

If you have any deep question, the escrow officer will direct you to your attorney. In MANY states in the USA, an attorney is mandatory in the closing process. (Not California)

Example - unless you have a trust, in California you might want the vesting on your real property to read:

Robert and Martha Smith, husband and wife, community property with right of survivorship.

Community Property means both of you have to sign to sell or transfer it at a later date – right of survivorship means should one die, the other inherits the property automatically with NO TAX consequences.

H.O.A – Home Owners Association

A homeowner's association (HOA) is an organization in a subdivision, planned community, or condominium building that makes and enforces rules for the properties and residents.

HOA is Home Owners Association, there are usually monthly HOA FEES that you must pay that range   from a couple hundred to a couple thousand, to many thousands of dollars, all are different.

ASK your realtor if there is HOA, read the listing online looking for HOA fee amount.

Some HOA's have annual fees some quarterly and some monthly. HOA's vary wildly in what value they provide to their members for their fees paid.

With some HOA's you are automatically a member of when you buy the property, others you have to be approved before you can close the deal to buy the property.

There may be other benefits and costs, ask lots of questions. Go meet the HOA president or leader.

Some HOA's fund things like recreation centers, swimming pools, parks, street lights, street paving, gate maintenance, all sorts of things that an HOA can have that all require fees to generate funds to keep it all going.

Interest Only Loans

There are limited mortgages out there where you pay interest only on a loan. This is a loan type that should only be considered in very limited situations such as bridge financing.

Let's say you have a property on the market, you're confident of the selling price, but it's not sold yet, or maybe it's not yet on the market and your dream house comes along.

Your finances might be tight, so you qualify for an interest-only loan for the new house until you sell the old house and roll your equity into the new house with a re-finance into a conventional mortgage....

This is risky, and should be given a lot of careful thought and I do not recommend doing anything risky.

Balloon Payments

There are loan programs out there that offer a lower interest rate for a limited time, or simply offer a loan for a limited time, at the end of which there is a large "balloon payment due.

Example, a 30-year amortized mortgage at 5% with a balloon payment due at 10 years. This means you make 10 years' worth of payments, then have to pay off the whole loan in one big payment.

Again, this can be very risky and should be given a lot of thought.

Sometimes experienced investors use this when they know that they will sell the property in an improved profitable state in a few years and they use this strategy to lower monthly payments.

The Offer

When you find a home you can afford, you and your realtor will create an offer. Your realtor will generate your offer on predefined real estate forms.

You will not only make a monetary offer as in how much you will pay, but also what you want…. i.e. – all appliances, a 1-year home warranty, a 30-day escrow, the neat bird bath in the back yard, all the trash removed from the basement, the tires behind the shed removed, etc.…. whatever you want included.

Your realtor will guide you, but if it's not on the offer, it does not exist. If you do not stipulate what appliances you want, they may disappear.

Everything you do will be in a written format, if it's not in writing, it does not exist.

Your offer will have an expiration date, usually 3 or 5 days for the seller to respond. You will need to attach your LOAN APPROVAL letter from your lender and an "Earnest Money" check…. Usually, $1 to $10,000.

If your offer is accepted your check is deposited to escrow, if not accepted, they return it uncashed. TRY to do a $1k check, this leaves more money in your bank account for lender to see.

IF the deal falls out, escrow returns your deposit. IF your offer is accepted, not only will your check be deposited but the clock will start ticking.

You will usually have 17 days for inspections, your realtor will help guide you as to who and what – you will pay for all this, of course.

Escrow will take over most of the timelines

Your realtor's computer will spit out many pages for you to sign and initial.

Read them.

If you are not familiar with what it means, ask. Your realtor's Broker knows every bit of real estate law should your realtor not have a good answer, that's the broker's job to keep their agents accurate.

Realtors are very busy, well paid and they will leave things blank on paperwork because they are always in a hurry.

Sellers hate this as they are basically asking a seller to agree to an incomplete contract.

Read and fully understand what you sign, ask that documents be complete before you sign.

Blanks that do not apply on documents should be market N/A (not applicable) or some such indicator that they are intentionally left blank.

Incomplete documents can create legal issues should you ever end up in court.

I am always ready to walk away from a deal if it's not clean and to my liking.

Inspections

AFTER your offer is accepted, you will be given 17 days to physically have access to and be able to inspect every part of the property.

Do not delay here, but this phase goes AFTER your offer is accepted. Should you find something bad, something you cannot live with, then you have the right to cancel the offer and get your money back IF it is done within the inspection period.

Your realtor will detail the timeline in the offer, it's important to understand this so go over it with your realtor before you sign and submit your offer.

You may well want to hire a professional home inspector. Home inspectors do a standardized battery of checks and document what they find as deficient. Today's home inspectors also scope the sewer main, and check all the plumbing.

Home inspectors do not check roofing, a licensed roofer will do this if you are concerned.

Home inspectors do not inspect areas they cannot get to, or get to safely.

If a home inspector has a concern, say a small crack in a foundation, they will recommend that you hire a licensed engineer to inspect and write an opinion to anything they cannot access or are not licensed to evaluate.

Some home inspection companies provide a warranty to the buyer, so that for a few years (plans differ) if something goes wrong, they will pay "so many" thousand dollars for the repairs if it was an item they missed during inspection.

Home warranties can be bought from insurance companies who specialize in this type product. Sometimes a home warranty is a good idea, especially for the first couple years. Houses are usually "used", similar to used cars they have wear and tear.

A PEST inspection, is usually required. A licensed pest control inspector will check the entire home for termites, rot, rodents and damage caused by pests.

IF they find a healthy, hungry colony of termites, they will advise how to treat them (kill) and this will need to be done, usually at sellers' expense, before your loan will fund and/or escrow close.

This treatment of pests can be as simple as some topical pesticide sprayed on directly, or a whole house tenting then fumigation with gas.

If a pest control company tents a house to fumigate termites, it kills all the landscaping next to the house, so sometimes you might want to just cancel the deal if the landscaping is not replaceable easily.

If they find rodents, they will advise extermination, then removal and close up their access.

Wood rot also known as dry rot, under a shower, under a roof, near the foundation and other locations can be very expensive as the only effective way to remedy it is to replace every rotten board.

A pest inspection includes finding dry rot and remediating it.

Many times, what is found in an inspection will be minor, and you have the option of asking the owner to correct, or just fix it yourself after close.

In my experience, the less you ask the owner to do, the more chance you deal will close… HOWEVER, you should be ready to cancel the deal and walk away if something big is found in the inspection.

There may be faults to a home that is for sale that cannot be corrected, or they are so expensive no one wants to do it.

It's important to hire qualified people to do your inspections unless you are qualified.

Cracked slab foundations, pipes leaking under a slab, unsafe construction or unsafe remodel work, and much more.

Always try to keep emotion out of the home purchase business, be prepared to walk away, after you close there will be much time to fall in love with the home.

After the close

Escrow's closing costs will include $$ that pay the part of the month you close in, and usually the first year's taxes.

Your first mortgage payment will be due the month after the month after you close, meaning you get a month with no payment! Which is good because most people are pretty broke by this time in the process!

You will write a check and mail it as your first mortgage payment to the lender who originated your loan, they always get the first payment as part of their compensation.

Then you will get a letter in the mail introducing you to the bank that has bought the servicing rights to your loan.

This new bank might be someone you have heard of, or some weird little bank in Mississippi who bid and won the servicing contract.

They will have a nice web site where you can set up your account and manage your loan.

Meanwhile Fannie Mae or Freddy Mac (whichever one bid and bought your mortgage from the originator) will be wrapping your debt into a mortgage-backed security (along with 10,000 other mortgages) and selling them on Wall Street to some greedy little fund manager.

You will make your payments, enjoy your house, and build wealth. You now own the best hedge against inflation there is while you enjoy the utility value of home sweet home.

I highly recommend, overpay the mortgage each month if you can, at least to the next highest hundred. Overpaying each month can take months off the back end.

Using your favorite web browser, you can giggle instructions how to build yourself an amortization schedule in something like MS-Excel, and then you can clearly see what a few extra bucks towards the principle of the mortgage does to the length of the term.

The home buying process – Detail

Usually, in this order – Many properties have issues unique to them that might change the below order of events.

One such thing might make the events different is if the property you are buying is in an H.O.A. (Home Owners Association) and the buyers must be approved by the HOA board to move into the neighborhood.

The below is an illustration of how it often goes, your deal may be different.

1) Know your numbers – i.e. – your Credit scores, your Income(s) and Expenses

2) Save money for down payment, appraisal, closing costs and moving expense

3) Select a lender and get a Pre-Approval letter

4) Decide WHERE you are willing to live. (Decide MAX commute distance, etc.)

5) Start watching REALTOR.COM - Review the areas you are interested in. I would set up an account, get the email of NEWEST listings in these areas daily. If something comes up in your price range, go look at it

6) After you find a property, you want to buy, you will make a written offer.

7) IF the seller chooses to, they can accept your offer, counter it, take someone else's offer or just let your offer expire.

8) IF the seller accepts your offer, they may accept with or without conditions. If there are conditions, you will need to decide if you are willing to accept them. You can counter offer, counter-counter… Etc. until everyone is happy or one party decides to walk away from the deal. Your realtor will help with this.

9) If you and Seller accept each other's written terms – then the seller's realtor opens Escrow with a Title Company

10) An Escrow agent will be assigned and she will contact you with lots of things you need to do quickly – be ready to respond, time is of the essence.

11) The escrow agent will set a target closing date – 45 to 90 days

12) Escrow will create "Escrow Instructions" that you and the seller will approve

13) Your Loan Agent will order an appraisal or the property

14) Your loan agent may suggest you "lock your rate" somewhere in this process to protect your rate from increasing. Your loan agent will explain this.

15) Sellers's disclosures will be provided to you, if not already provided.

16) A "preliminary Title" report will be pulled by escrow and provided to you for approval

17) A flood report will be pulled to see if your lender will require you to buy flood insurance.

18) If you are having a property inspection, that will be scheduled.

19) Your loan Agent will request all your documentation to move the loan towards approval

20) You will electronically submit all documentation requested by your loan agent

21) The loan agent will submit all your completed documentation to "underwriting" (Underwriting is the group that approves or denies the loan, they live in a secret cave deep in the arctic where no borrowers can ever speak to them – Your loan agent is your only communicator between you and "underwriting")

22) Underwriting MAY or MAY NOT have questions on your documentation, you will answer all questions with more supporting evidence or sometimes just a letter stating the facts.

23) The appraisal will come in telling the lender what the house is worth today

24) IF the house "appraises" the loan moves forward – or deal dies.

25) Escrow will then generate a document called "Estimated Closing costs"

26) You will deposit your down payment and estimated closing costs into Escrow Account

27) When Escrow has cleared all title issues, then they will "close' escrow

28) Title Insurance will be issued (this insures the lender against title defects)

29) Title will be transferred into your name

30) Any walk through with seller (if needed or requested) will then occur

31) Final walk-through with your realtor

32) Your realtor gives you the keys to your home!

33) You move in, change the locks and your life's journey adds another chapter!

Reviewing your credit scores

To start with let's look at the 5 levels of credit scores with a description of what they mean.

Exceptional: 800 to 850.

Very good: 740 to 799.

Good: 670 to 739.

Fair: 580 to 669.

Poor: 300 to 579.

You ideally want a credit score of 740 or higher before you apply for a mortgage as this will get you a loan that has favorable terms for the borrower.

Financial institutions like to deal with people who have higher scores as the likelihood of the borrower paying their debt is higher.

However, people with lower scores, well they pay a lot more, so banks like them too, but only to a point.

Many financial institutions bundle borrowers' debt and sell it to the investment market.

When they bundle loans and sell them, they represent to the investors that buy the debt what the borrower classes credit worthiness is, the better your score, and the rest of the borrowers in the debt pool they are bundling and selling, the more value (money) the bank gets when they sell your debt (if they do).

Like almost everything in life, there are at least 2 sides to look at – in the credit market, there is the borrower's perspective and then there is the lenders.

Sometimes understanding both sides or the other side of a deal, can help you a lot.

Personally, I never want to pay more for something than I have to, so I have taken care of my credit to keep my interest rates low.

Having a great credit score will save you money EVERY month on your mortgage.

A favorable high score can not only help you get a loan, but literally save thousands of dollars every year. Low credit may mean no mortgage, as in "DENIED", or it may mean they offer you a "special deal" where in they charge you lots more and let you know they are doing you a favor….

It really is worthwhile to take some time and try to improve your scores BEFORE you apply for a mortgage.

Do not forget, if you are applying for credit with another person, i.e. - spouse, partner, parent, etc. Your co-applicant(s) score(s) matter to as the lender will include their score into the approval process.

It is also worthwhile to take some time and try to improve your co-applicants scores BEFORE you apply for a mortgage, and/or at least know what they are.

A perfect credit score today is 850.

Earning an "850" takes a while (and age), income, responsible credit use and a lot of diligence.

Credit scores are something many people do not understand. MOST people think it's just how much you earn…. Not so, there are 2 equally important parts.

KNOW your credit report and your scores!

Creditability and willingness to pay

There are people who have the "creditability" aspect of credit worthiness as in high income or liquid assets, but if they don't pay their bills on time, their "willingness to pay "is very poor, and earns them a poor credit rating.

If you don't respect your creditors they won't respect you, but they will extend you credit and they will charge you lots of interest, late fees, overdraft fees, and anything else they can stick you with.

You can make $500k a year and have a poor credit score because you're a stoop who does not pay their bills on time. Although you might, in this example, have great income, you are viewed as irresponsible. No one wants that sophomoric label.

Creditability is the amount you earn vs. amount of credit you have available   and Willingness to pay is how faithfully you pay on time as agreed. This shows how responsible you are and demonstrates respect for your lenders.

ANY time you apply for credit, your score is temporarily reduced. As part of preparing to get a mortgage, try really hard not to apply for new credit the months prior

This includes buying that new "free" smartphone – the "free" one your cellular carrier tucks 26 bucks a month onto your bill for – when you get a new phone, they run your credit, and this can reduce your score temporarily.

Credit card applications, new cable service, new apartment, new job, etc. can trigger a credit check and lower your score.

The lower your score, the higher your mortgage rate – or flat-out denial. A half percent higher mortgage can cost you tens of thousands of dollars over the life of the loan

When you pick a mortgage company, stick with them so your credit report is only pulled ONCE.

Applying to 3 different mortgage companies at the same time can cost you 100 points as to the rating services it looks like your desperate for a loan.

It's also prudent to avoid cancelling any credit while you are preparing to get a loan, this will LOWER your score.

Yep, canceling existing credit lowers your score!

For instance, I recently fired Bank of America as I do not like their political involvements – I don't do business with any financial institution that gets political.

I called B of A, and I cancelled the 4 credit card accounts I had with them.

Now truth be known, I have not used these much in years. I ended up with 4 separate visa card accounts as B of A acquired 3 other banks that I had previous relationships with.

After canceling these 4 accounts, my score dropped from 848 to 827, 3 months later it was back at 849.

This reduction of my borrowing power, reduced my credit score. (Temporarily i.e. - a few months)

If I was near a border say between "Good" and "Fair" credit, canceling credit could have pushed me down into "Fair".

If I was applying for a mortgage and my credit rating dropped to "Fair", it would cost me money as in a higher payment every month.

Never cancel credit without thinking it through.

How to improve your credit score

Credit reporting in The United States is governed by federal law, specifically 15 U.S.C. §§ 1681-1681x, et al. § 605 contains the requirements relating to information contained in consumer reports [15 U.S.C. § 1681c].

If you are interested to learn more, do a web search on 15 USC and find the sections that are The Fair Credit Reporting Act of 1996. It's an interesting read to be sure.

An easy way to improve your score fast, is to OVER PAY every minimum payment by at least a dollar each month. When I did this, I went from a 760 to 850 in 2 months.

But before that I had to get to 760. That required a few years of carefully using my credit, not being late and not getting in over my head with payments vs/ my income.

It's a good idea to always use your credit carefully and wisely.

My grandfather always said, "if you can't pay cash for something, you cannot afford it". OK, but that was a long time ago, and today credit use is a part of almost everyone's successful life.

When credit is used responsibly and in moderation, meaning in concert with your income and income source stability, it can help you in a lot of ways, such as buying a house!

Never Ever be late with any payment, that's the fastest way to diminish your credit score

For myself, I never extended any credit card to its maximum. I never extended credit cards to the point I could not afford to pay them off in 12 months.

The amounts of interest most credit cards charge you is very high, so the repayment is very expensive.

There are lots of online services available today... Personally I don't trust them much as they are mostly intermediatory services and as such you never know who you are really sharing personal financial information with online.

The 3 official credit reporting agencies are:

Experian - https://www.experian.com/

Equifax - https://www.equifax.com

Trans Union - https://www.transunion.com

Each of these official agencies have online access portals that I do trust.

I have a login and access to all 3 credit reporting agencies. I trust them by working directly.

An approach to improve your credit scores is to start by pulling your credit report from ALL three credit agencies so you know EXACTLY what information they hold on you before you apply for a mortgage.

When you get your credit report from each agency, the format will be a bit different, but they each will include instructions on how to read the report they sent you.

Credit Reports can be confusing at first, sometimes if you have a lot of credit history the report can be overwhelming, but I have confidence you will figure it out.

Should there be anything negative, try to have it removed before you apply for a mortgage.

You will find a way to contest the validity of an entry via each of the reporting agencies websites.

Do not be surprised if you find several wrong spellings of your name, social security #, etc.

Data is only as good as it is collected and entered. Mistakes happen during entry and it's a good idea to correct them.

If you cannot have it removed, then be prepared to explain to a future lender in a business-like fashion why the event occurred and why it will not happen again.

There are timelines that credit reporting agencies must, by law, adhere to verify any item or otherwise remove the item from your record.

In conclusion to all the above

Owning your own home, having a place to call your own is a cornerstone of the American dream.

In today's world, I believe anyone who works hard, plans ahead, is honest and diligently continues to work hard can succeed in attaining this part of the American Dream.

Always understand what you are signing before you sign anything.

If need be, get an attorney's advice. Listen to your realtor. If you don't trust your realtor, get a different one you do trust.

CPA's can answer tax related questions, if you are concerned about any part of what you are buying, get a licensed professional to do an inspection – do not skimp on paying for inspections.

As a homeowner, you will hopefully feel a pride of ownership, a freedom and a sense of major accomplishment.

Plan ahead and remember, often the journey is as exciting as the destination.

I wish everyone the very best always.

About the Author

The accumulation of 35 years buying and selling Real Estate – Stephen shares his firsthand knowledge to help you understand the real estate process so you too can succeed with this experienced based book about real estate buying.

When buying Real Property, such as a home, there is a process that you will navigate, it's pretty well defined and this book is intended to help enlighten you to help you navigate the process, by sharing knowledge

Buying a home can be very stressful, but knowledge helps alleviate this stress and can make the journey towards homeownership rewarding.